WORKING FOR PATIENTS

Foreword by the Prime Minister

"The National Health Service at its best is without equal. Time and again, the nation has seen just how much we owe to those who work in it.

"A skilled and dedicated staff - backed by enormously increased resources - have coped superbly with the growing demands of modern medicine and increasing numbers of patients. There is a great deal of which we can all feel very proud.

"The National Health Service will continue to be available to all, regardless of income, and to be financed mainly out of general taxation.

"But major tasks now face us: to bring all parts of the National Health Service up to the very high standard of the best, while maintaining the principles on which it was founded; and to prepare for the needs of the future.

"We aim to extend patient choice, to delegate responsibility to where the services are provided and to secure the best value for money.

"All the proposals in this White Paper put the needs of patients first.

"They apply to the whole of the United Kingdom but there are separate chapters on Scotland, Wales and Northern Ireland to cater for their special circumstances.

"We believe that a National Health Service that is run better, will be a National Health Service that can care better.

"Taken together, the proposals represent the most far-reaching reform of the National Health Service in its forty year history.

"They offer new opportunities, and pose new challenges, for everyone concerned with the running of the Service.

"I am confident that all who work in it will grasp these opportunities to provide even better health care for the millions and millions of people who rely on the National Health Service.

"The patient's needs will always be paramount."

Margaret Thatcher

CONTENTS

PART ONE: THE GOVERNMENT'S STRATEGY

CHAPTER 1:

A BETTER
HEALTH
SERVICE
FOR PATIENTS

INTRODUCTION

The achievements of the NHS

1.1 The United Kingdom enjoys high standards of health care. The Health Service has contributed to longer life expectancy, fewer stillbirths and lower rates of perinatal and infant mortality. There have been dramatic increases in the number of people treated in hospital. Transplant surgery is now commonplace. Doctors can carry out successful hip operations on people in their seventies and eighties. People are not only living longer but are enjoying a better quality of life.

1.2 The proposals in this White Paper aim to build on these achievements by providing an even better service for patients. To do that the Government will keep all that is best in the NHS. The principles which have guided it for the last 40 years will continue to guide it into the twenty-first century. The NHS is, and will continue to be, open to all, regardless of income, and financed mainly out of general taxation.

1.3 The NHS is growing at a truly remarkable pace. The number of hospital doctors and dentists has increased from 42,000 in 1978 to over 48,000 in 1987, and the number of nursing and midwifery staff from 444,000 to 514,000. Total gross expenditure will increase from £8 billion in 1978-79 to £26 billion in 1989-90, an increase of 40 per cent after allowing for general inflation. Expenditure by the NHS will then be equivalent to around £35 a week for an average family of four, as compared with about £11 in 1978-79. This and improved productivity mean, to take just one example, that NHS hospital staff now treat over one and a half million more in-patients a year than in 1978, bringing the total to nearly eight million.

The need for change

1.4 Throughout the 1980s the Government has thus presided over a massive expansion of the NHS. It has ensured that the quality of care provided and the response to emergencies remain among the best in the world. But it has become increasingly clear that more needs to be done because of rising demand and an ever-widening range of treatments made possible by advances in medical technology. It has also increasingly been recognised that simply injecting more and more money is not, by itself, the answer.

1.5 It is clear that the organisation of the NHS - the way it delivers health care to the individual patient - also needs to be reformed. The Government has been tackling these organisational problems, and has taken a series of measures to improve the way the NHS is managed. The main one was the introduction of general management from 1984. This is now showing results and has pointed the way ahead.

1.6 New management information systems have provided clear evidence of a wide variation in performance up and down the country. In 1986-87, the average cost of treating acute hospital in-patients varied by as much as 50 per cent between different health authorities, even after allowing for the complexity and mix of cases treated. Similarly, a patient who waits several years for an operation in one place may get that same operation within a few weeks in another. There are wide variations in the drug prescribing habits of GPs, and in some places drug costs are nearly twice as high per head of population as in others. And, at the extremes, there is a twenty-fold variation in the rate at which GPs refer patients to hospital.

1.7 The Government wants to raise the performance of all hospitals and GP practices to that of the best. The main question it has addressed in its review of the NHS has been how best to achieve that. It is convinced that it can be done only by delegating responsibility as closely as possible to where health care is delivered to the patient - predominantly to the GP and the local hospital. Experience in both the public service and the private sector has shown that the best run services are those in which local staff are given responsibility for responding to local needs.

1.8 This White Paper presents a programme of action, summarised in chapter 13, to secure two objectives:

• to give patients, wherever they live in the UK, better health care and greater choice of the services available; and

- greater satisfaction and rewards for those working in the NHS who successfully respond to local needs and preferences.

THE GOVERNMENT'S PROPOSALS

Key changes

1.9 The Government is proposing seven key measures to achieve these objectives:

First: **to make the Health Service more responsive to the needs of patients, as much power and responsibility as possible will be delegated to local level.** This includes the delegation of functions from Regions to Districts, and from Districts to hospitals. The detailed proposals are set out in the next chapter. They include greater flexibility in setting the pay and conditions of staff, and financial incentives to make the best use of a hospital's assets.

Second: **to stimulate a better service to the patient, hospitals will be able to apply for a new self-governing status as NHS Hospital Trusts.** This means that, while remaining within the NHS, they will take fuller responsibility for their own affairs, harnessing the skills and dedication of their staff. NHS Hospital Trusts will earn revenue from the services they provide. They will therefore have an incentive to attract patients, so they will make sure that the service they offer is what their patients want. And in turn they will stimulate other NHS hospitals to respond to what people want locally. NHS Hospital Trusts will also be able to set the rates of pay of their own staff and, within annual financing limits, to borrow money to help them respond to patient demand.

Third: **to enable hospitals which best meet the needs and wishes of patients to get the money to do so, the money required to treat patients will be able to cross administrative boundaries.** All NHS hospitals, whether run by health authorities or self-governing, will be free to offer their services to different health authorities and to the private sector. Consequently, a health authority will be better able to discharge its duty to use its available funds to secure a comprehensive service, including emergency services, by obtaining the best service it can whether from its own hospitals, from another authority's hospitals, from NHS Hospital Trusts or from the private sector.

Fourth: **to reduce waiting times and improve the quality of service, to help give individual patients appointment times they can rely on, and to help cut the long hours worked by some junior doctors, 100 new consultant posts will be created over the next three years.** This is in line with the number of fully trained doctors ready for consultant appointments in the relevant specialties. The new posts will be additional to the two per cent annual expansion of consultant numbers already planned.

Fifth: **to help the family doctor improve his service to patients, large GP practices will be able to apply for their own budgets to obtain a defined range of services direct from hospitals.** Again, in the interests of a better service to the patient, GPs will be encouraged to compete for patients by offering better services. And it will be easier for patients to choose (and change) their own GP as they wish.

Sixth: **to improve the effectiveness of NHS management, regional, district and family practitioner management bodies will be reduced in size and reformed on business lines, with executive and non-executive directors.** The Government believes that, in the interests of patients and staff, the era in which a £26 billion NHS is run by authorities which are neither truly representative nor fully management bodies must be ended. The confusion of roles will be replaced by a clear remit and accountability.

Seventh: **to ensure that all concerned with delivering services to the patient make the best use of the resources available to them, quality of service and value for money will be more rigorously audited.** Arrangements for what doctors call "medical audit" will be extended throughout the Health Service, helping to ensure that the best quality of medical care is given to patients. The Audit Commission will assume responsibility for auditing the accounts of health authorities and other NHS bodies, and will undertake wide-ranging value for money studies.

1.10 The Secretary of State for Health will publish shortly eight working papers explaining in detail how major aspects of the Government's proposals are to be implemented in England, as a basis for discussion with interested parties. Similar papers will be published as necessary by the Secretaries of State for Scotland, Wales and Northern Ireland.

Putting patients first

1.11 While the purpose of all the reforms in this White Paper is to provide a better service for patients, some will take time to work through. In the meantime the Government will expect health authorities to take more direct action on a number of fronts to tackle the problems of greatest public concern.

1.12 People still sometimes have to wait too long for treatment, and may have little if any choice over the time or place at which treatment is given. The Government has already done much to tackle this problem. Over the past two years, £64 million has been spent on a new initiative to reduce waiting lists and waiting times, allowing over 230,000 additional patients to be treated. Half of all waiting list patients are now admitted from the list within five weeks or less. In 1989-90, another £40 million will be spent on this initiative.

1.13 At present the service provided on admission to hospital is sometimes too impersonal and inflexible. This is not what either the Government or those working in the Health Service want to see. The best NHS hospitals provide more than clinical excellence. They provide a service which considers patients as people. The Government is determined that this is what all hospitals should provide. It believes that each hospital should offer:

- appointments systems which give people individual appointment times that they can rely on. Waits of two to three hours in out-patient clinics are unacceptable.

- quiet and pleasant waiting and other public areas, with proper facilities for parents with children and for counselling worried parents and relatives.

- clear information leaflets about the facilities available and what patients need to know when they come into hospital.

- clearer, easier and more sensitive procedures for making suggestions for improvements and, if necessary, complaints.

- once someone is in hospital, clear and sensitive explanations of what is happening - on practical matters, such as where to go and who to see, and on clinical matters, such as the nature of an illness and its proposed treatment.

- rapid notification of the results of diagnostic tests.

- a wider range of optional extras and amenities for patients who want to pay for them - such as single rooms, personal telephones, televisions, and a wider choice of meals.

1.14 In short, every hospital in the NHS should offer what the best offer now. These improvements will bring greater appreciation and recognition from patients and their families for all the care that the Health Service provides.

The best use of resources

1.15 If the NHS is to provide the best service it can for its patients, it must make the best use of the resources available to it. The quest for value for money must be an essential element in its work. This becomes even more important as the demands on the Health Service continue to grow.

1.16 Those who take decisions which involve spending money must be accountable for that spending. Equally, those who are responsible for managing the service must be able to influence the way in which its resources are used. The Government believes that most decisions are better taken at local level. Parts Two and Three of this White Paper include a range of important proposals for strengthening local management and improving value for money in addition to those referred to in paragraph 1.9. They build on the introduction of general management and on the proposals for the better management of the family practitioner services (FPS) set out in "Promoting Better Health" (Cm 249).

1.17 Among the most important aims behind these changes are:

- to secure a clearer distinction at national level between the policy responsibilities of Ministers and the operational responsibilities of the Chief Executive and top management;

- to improve the information available to local managers, enabling them in turn to make their budgeting and monitoring more accurate, sensitive and timely;

- to ensure that hospital consultants - whose decisions effectively commit substantial sums of money - are involved in the management of hospitals; are given responsibility for the use of resources; and are encouraged to use those resources more effectively;

- to contract out more functions which do not have to be undertaken by health authority staff and which could be provided more cost effectively by the private sector; and

- to ensure that drug prescribing costs are kept within reasonable limits.

Public and private sectors working together

1.18 The NHS and the independent health sector should be able to learn from each other, to support each other and to provide services for each other. Anyone needing treatment can only benefit from such a development. People who choose to buy health care outside the Health Service benefit the community by taking pressure off the Service and add to the diversity of provision and choice. The Government expects to see further increases in the number of people wishing to make private provision for health care, but at the moment many people who do so during their working life find the cost of higher premiums difficult to meet in retirement. The Government therefore proposes to make it easier for people in retirement by allowing income tax relief on their private medical insurance premiums, whether paid by them or, for example, by their families on their behalf.

Scope of proposals

1.19 The White Paper's proposals apply throughout the UK. The way in which they are implemented in England, Scotland, Wales and Northern Ireland will need to reflect the different organisational structures that have grown up in each country, in the light of their own distinctive health care needs and circumstances. Chapters 2-9 are written in terms which apply primarily to England. Those aspects which are particular to the other three countries are dealt with in chapters 10-12.

PART TWO: THE HOSPITAL SERVICE

- Now that general management is established, the Government is taking the next logical steps by delegating as much decision-making as possible to the local level. Hospitals and other management units will be expected to carry more direct responsibility for running their affairs. This has implications for the role of the centre and of Regional and District Health Authorities (RHAs and DHAs). It means giving hospitals greater control over, and better information about, their use of resources. (Chapter 2.)

- Hospitals will be able to opt for a new self-governing status while remaining in the NHS. Major acute hospitals are the obvious candidates but others may become self-governing in due course. (Chapter 3.)

- At the same time, the Government wants to create more incentives to better performance by changing the way in which hospitals are funded. At present, hospitals which offer the best value for money are often not rewarded for doing so. Indeed, hospitals may be penalised for their efficiency if they succeed in treating more patients than they had budgeted for. The Government intends to reverse this situation by ensuring that money flows to those hospitals which treat most patients. (Chapter 4.)

- Delegation downwards must be matched by accountability upwards. General managers are already formally accountable for the spending of their health authorities, but it is hospital consultants whose decisions in practice determine how a hospital's resources are used. It is therefore important to ensure that consultants are given more responsibility for their use of resources. (Chapter 5.)

CHAPTER 2

INTRODUCTION

2.1   Since taking office, much of the Government's policy has been aimed at strengthening the management of the hospital service and improving its performance through the better use of resources. These changes have helped to improve efficiency throughout the hospital service, and to generate additional revenue from cash-releasing cost improvements amounting to over £900 million a year by 1988-89. In addition, receipts from land sales should exceed £300 million this year.

2.2   The running of the hospital service cannot however be administered in detail from Whitehall by Ministers or by civil servants. The Government's main task must be to set a national framework of objectives and priorities. Local management must then be allowed to get on with the task of managing, while remaining accountable to the centre for its delivery of the Government's objectives.

DELEGATING RESPONSIBILITY

Central management of the NHS

2.3   The NHS will continue to be funded by the Government mainly from tax revenues. Ministers must be accountable to Parliament and to the public for the spending of these huge sums of money. Such accountability does not mean that Ministers should be involved in operational decisions. On the contrary, these decisions must be taken locally by operational units with Ministers being responsible for policy and strategy.

2.4   The central management of the NHS must reflect this division of responsibilities. The Government proposes that responsibility for strategy will be for an NHS Policy Board chaired by the Secretary of State for Health. Responsibility for all operational matters will be for an NHS Management Executive chaired by a Chief Executive. The Management Executive will be accountable to the Policy Board for the management of the NHS within the strategy and objectives set by the Policy Board.

2.5   The specific proposals are:

- a new NHS Policy Board, chaired and appointed by the Secretary of State, will determine the strategy, objectives and finances of the NHS in the light of Government policy, and will set objectives for the NHS Management Executive and monitor whether they are satisfactorily achieved. It will replace the former Health Service Supervisory Board and will include non-executive members drawn from inside and outside the NHS.

- The NHS Management Executive will be chaired by the Chief Executive and appointed by the Secretary of State in consultation with the Chief Executive. It will deal with all operational matters within the strategy and objectives set by the Policy Board.

- Responsibility for the management of family practitioner services will be brought under the NHS Management Executive. The better integration of primary care and hospital services is an important objective.

2.6   The overall effect of these changes will be to introduce for the first time a clear and effective chain of management command running from Districts through Regions to the Chief Executive and from there to the Secretary of State.

The role of Regions

2.7   The NHS Management Executive could not directly exercise effective authority over the current 190 District Health Authorities (DHAs). Regional Health Authorities (RHAs) will therefore continue to ensure that Government policies are properly carried out within their Regions. To be effective, they will need to concentrate their efforts on their essential tasks. These include setting performance criteria, monitoring the performance of the Health Service and evaluating its effectiveness. They will have a key role to play in managing the wider programme of changes that are set out in this White Paper.

2.8   In addition, RHAs have traditionally provided a range of operational and management services. These include distribution centres, ambulance services and blood transfusion services which could not be provided economically in every District. They also include legal, information and management services to Districts themselves. Following the introduction of general management and the re-organisation of Regional headquarters, many RHAs have reviewed the provision of these services. As a result, some services have already been streamlined, delegated to Districts or contracted out to the private sector.

2.9   There remains, however, a wide variation in the size of each Region's operations. The Government believes that there is still considerable scope for reductions in the number of staff directly employed by RHAs on these operations. The NHS Management Executive will therefore review the provision of all regionally managed services. It will approve the retention of services at the Regional level only if it is cost-effective to do so. As part of this exercise, Districts will be asked whether they can provide more of these services themselves or purchase them from the private sector.

The role of Districts and hospitals

2.10   The Government also believes that there is further scope for delegating decision-making from DHAs to hospitals and their associated management units. Many large hospitals already have a significant degree of self-determination. RHAs will be expected to satisfy themselves that, wherever possible, all DHAs delegate operational functions to their hospitals, taking account of the availability of staff in key disciplines and the need to ensure that, overall, the management of services remains cost-effective.

2.11   The Government's objective is to create an organisation in which those who are actually providing the services are also responsible for day-to-day decisions about operational matters. Like RHAs, DHAs can then concentrate on ensuring that the health needs of the population for which they are responsible are met; that there are effective services for the prevention and control of diseases and the promotion of health; that their population has access to a comprehensive range of high quality, value for money services; and on setting targets for and monitoring the performance of those management units for which they continue to have responsibility. The Government will expect authorities to provide themselves with the medical and nursing advice they will need if they are to undertake these tasks effectively.

MANAGING RESOURCES

Better use of staff

2.12 One of the keys to successful management of the NHS is good management of people. Chapter 5 includes proposals for ensuring that consultants are involved in the management of hospitals and are given responsibility for the use of resources. But it is nurses who represent the largest single group of professional staff in the NHS and who are responsible for delivering direct patient care around the clock.

2.13 There have been many developments in recent years in the better use of nursing staff, but the Government believes that there is still scope for more progress at local level. It has already endorsed the need to provide better training for the non-professional support staff to nurses. As part of this initiative, local managers, in consultation with their professional colleagues, will be expected to re-examine all areas of work to identify the most cost-effective use of professional skills. This may involve a reappraisal of traditional patterns and practices. Examples include the extended role of nurses to cover specific duties normally undertaken by junior doctors in areas of high technology care and in casualty departments; the use of clerical rather than nursing staff in receptionist work; and making full use of midwives as recommended in the reports of the Maternity Services Advisory Committee. There is also scope for more cost-effective working in other professions, some of which, such as physiotherapists, speech therapists and chiropodists, make little use of non-professional helpers.

Better information

2.14 The Government recognises that managers and professional staff need better information if they are to make the best use of the resources that are available to them. The NHS has made considerable progress in developing better information systems in hospitals, but there remain some important limitations. In particular, there is at present only a limited capacity to link information about the diagnosis of patients and the cost of treatment. The Government believes that the best way to remedy this is by extending and accelerating the existing Resource Management Initiative (RMI). This is intended to provide a complete picture of the resources used in treating hospital patients. A key feature of the RMI is that doctors, nurses and other professional staff have much more information at their fingertips about the care their patients are getting. Their involvement in the development of the RMI has also ensured that the new systems are actively used for the benefit of patients.

2.15 In order to encourage further the involvement of doctors and nurses in management, the Government proposes to implement the RMI programme in England in two stages:

- during 1989, to extend preparation for the RMI in up to 50 acute hospital units, linked to improvements in the coding of medical records and experimentation in analysing activity data into case-mix groups. This stage is aimed at producing activity data that can be used, for example, for medical audit purposes.

- starting late in 1989, to extend the full RMI process to 20 acute hospital units with the aim of building up coverage to 260 acute units by the end of 1991-92.

2.16 This is an ambitious timetable, but the Government remains committed to introducing modern information systems to support both clinical and operational functions in hospitals.

Pay flexibility

2.17 In addition to giving managers the tools with which to manage, the Government wants to give them greater control over the resources for which they are responsible. Pay accounts for over 70 per cent of all NHS expenditure. Getting pay wrong can have serious effects on expenditure on the one hand, and on the availability of staff on the other.

2.18 Chapter 3 proposes that NHS Hospital Trusts should be free to settle the pay of their staff. But the Government's objective throughout the Service is progressively to introduce greater flexibility, in order to allow managers to relate pay rates to local labour markets and to reward individual performance.

2.19 Until recently, there has been no geographical variation of pay (other than London weighting) for NHS staff. The Nurses Pay Review Body, in its 1988 report, recommended London supplements to be paid in addition to London weighting to nurses and the professions allied to medicine, and these were introduced from 1 April 1988. The Government has now asked the Review Body to accept the case for more local discretionary payments to nurses to help with particular local staff shortages and nurse management problems.

2.20 The performance pay arrangements which apply to general managers and other top managers are being extended to senior and middle managers lower down the scale. The extended arrangements, unlike the original ones, include an explicit local flexibility element for posts at these levels, so that managers can react to local recruitment problems.

2.21 Negotiations are already under way to introduce flexibility into the administrative and clerical pay scales. This will be based on a national pay spine, but will allow local discretion to take account of market conditions.

Conditions of service

2.22 The Government also wants to give local managers greater flexibility to determine the conditions of service of NHS staff. This will enable them to devise employment packages that are most suited to local needs. At present, conditions of service are determined mainly by national negotiations in the Whitley Councils. An internal review of conditions of service by the Department of Health is nearing completion.

Capital

2.23 Managers should also be able to make the most efficient use of their physical resources. Capital in the NHS has been treated for the most part as a "free good". Once an investment has been made, whether in land, buildings or equipment, no further revenue charges arise from the continuing use of these capital assets. This can lead to inefficiency such as the under-utilisation of assets, and may also mean that capital costs are not fully taken into account when, for example, comparisons of cost and performance are made between different parts of the NHS, or with the private sector.

2.24 The Government proposes to introduce a new system of charging for capital in the NHS. From April 1991, health authorities will be charged for the use of their existing capital assets and any new capital investment. The charges will be set to cover the costs of interest and depreciation. Revenue allocations from Regions to Districts will be increased to cover the initial cost of the charges. Future capital investment will incur additional charges. The capital charging and funding system will be designed so that there is no net increase in public expenditure in the NHS and no reductions in the funds available for patient services. The charging system will provide a strong incentive for every authority to use its assets efficiently and to invest wisely. It will also place NHS hospitals on a more level footing with private hospitals, which have to meet the costs of capital on a normal, commercial basis. The Secretary of State will publish shortly a working paper which will set out the detail of how the capital charging scheme will be implemented, as a basis for discussion with interested parties.

2.25 Funds for capital investment will continue to be financed by the Exchequer and , except for NHS Hospital Trusts, will be allocated by RHAs from within an overall capital programme. There will therefore continue to be strategic oversight of capital planning, within an overall cash limit. But the capital charging scheme will ensure that managers are given clear financial signals when taking decisions on capital deployment.

2.26 There are opportunities for health authorities to derive income and large capital sums from property which is surplus to requirements. There is little experience in the NHS of undertaking complex and specialised property transactions. Indeed, health authorities may only encounter this occasionally. In order to assist them in this, the NHS will in future be able to call on the advice of a central group of professionals, including members drawn from the private sector with the necessary property, financial and legal expertise.

2.27 The Government also intends to delegate more decisions about individual capital schemes. The expenditure limits above which projects have to be referred centrally for approval will therefore be increased. From now on only schemes with a capital cost of over £10m (previously £5m) will be referred to the Department of Health for approval. Of these, only those over £15m (previously £10m) will be referred to the Treasury. These increases will be a welcome step forward in speeding up investment approvals and giving health service managers greater freedom over key resource decisions.

Private capital

2.28 As health authorities become more business-like in their approach to the provision of services, and to the use of the resources at their disposal, they are increasingly looking at the scope for involving the private sector. Examples include joint ventures where the NHS provides land and a developer puts up a building, or where a major service is contracted out to the private sector. There may also be opportunities for an authority to work with a private developer to achieve a net saving. The Government is determined to encourage these schemes whenever they are consistent with value for money and the proper control of public expenditure.

2.29 To assist in the aim of achieving better value for money, the Government intends also to make changes in the arrangements for audit. At present, the statutory external audit of the accounts of the health authorities and Family Practitioner Committees (FPCs) is carried out by the Health Departments. The Government's objective is that there should be more commitment to value for money studies, which would cover a wider range of NHS activity, by an audit body that is demonstrably independent of the health authorities and FPCs, and of the Health Departments.

2.30 Accordingly, the Government proposes to transfer responsibility for the statutory external audit in England and Wales to an independent body, the Audit Commission. The Audit Commission is currently responsible for the audit of local authorities in England and Wales; these audits are carried out by a mixture of the Commission's own staff and private sector firms. The Commission has considerable experience and expertise in areas of work closely related to the Health Service. In particular, it is accustomed to working in multi-disciplinary teams with professionals looking at the professional aspects of services. This will mean the involvement of independent professionals in audit work and will be an important part of the Commission's new role in the Health Service.

2.31 The Local Government and Housing Bill to be published soon after this White Paper will include a provision which will enable the Audit Commission to undertake audit in the NHS under authority of the Secretary of State. This will develop the experience of the Audit Commission, and enable its staff to start to work with the officials in the Department of Health and Welsh Office who are currently responsible for NHS audit. The Government intends to bring forward further legislation formally establishing the Audit Commission as the body responsible for the external audit of health authorities and other NHS bodies in England and Wales which are at present audited by the Department of Health and the Welsh Office. In this capacity, it would report to the appropriate Secretary of State. It is also likely that the bulk of the staff of the present NHS statutory audit service, who are civil servants and employees of the Department of Health and Welsh Office, will transfer to the Audit Commission. In this way there will be continuity of expertise in the audit of the NHS.

2.32 The responsibilities of the Audit Commission will cover the full range of organisations within the NHS as they develop, including the proposed NHS Hospital Trusts and GP practice budgets. It will provide an independent source of advice to Ministers. Its reports will be published under the authority of the Secretaries of State for Health and for Wales, and will be made available to Parliament and the public.

2.33 The role of the National Audit Office will remain unchanged. As an Officer of Parliament, the Comptroller and Auditor General will continue to report on value for money in the use of voted funds, and to certify the aggregated accounts of the NHS, drawing upon the audits carried out by the Audit Commission, just as at present he draws upon the audits carried out by the Health Departments.

CHAPTER 3

INTRODUCTION

3.1   This chapter sets out the Government's proposals for enabling as many hospitals as are willing and able to do so to run their own affairs, whilst remaining in the NHS.

3.2   The Government expects that major acute hospitals will be the most suitable candidates for its proposals, but other hospitals may also come within their scope. There are currently over 320 major acute hospitals in the UK - "major" defined as having more than 250 beds. These are substantial enterprises. Even the smallest of the management units which currently run these hospitals may have revenue budgets in excess of £10 million a year. The largest may have budgets in excess of £50 million. Some of these hospitals already have substantial responsibilities delegated to them for running their own affairs. The Government intends to take this process much further by providing for a full, self-governing status for hospitals.

3.3   The Government believes that self-government for hospitals will encourage a stronger sense of local ownership and pride, building on the enormous fund of goodwill that exists in local communities. It will stimulate the commitment and harness the skills of those who are directly responsible for providing services. Supported by a funding system in which successful hospitals can flourish, it will encourage local initiative and greater competition. All this in turn will ensure a better deal for the public, improving the choice and quality of the services offered and the efficiency with which those services are delivered.

NHS HOSPITAL TRUSTS

3.4   The powers and responsibilities of each self-governing hospital will need to be formally vested in a new and separate legal body, to be known as an NHS Hospital Trust. Each NHS Hospital Trust will be run by a board of directors. The Government will bring forward legislation enabling the Secretary of State to establish NHS Hospital Trusts and to appoint their boards. The Government proposes that the board of directors of an NHS Hospital Trust should be constituted as follows:

- There will be a balanced number of executive and non-executive directors and, in addition, a non-executive chairman.

- No board will have more than ten directors, excluding the chairman.

- The chairman will be appointed by the Secretary of State.

- Of the non-executive directors at least two will be drawn from the local community, for example from hospital Leagues of Friends and similar organisations. These two "community" directors will be appointed by the Regional Health Authority (RHA). The remaining non-executive directors will be appointed by the Secretary of State after consulting the chairman. All the non-executive directors will be chosen for the contribution they personally can make to the effective management of the hospital and not for any interest group which they might represent. None will be an employee of a health authority or hospital, of a trade union with members who work in the NHS, or of a major contractor or other hospital supplier. For teaching hospitals, the non-executive directors will need to include someone drawn from the relevant medical school.

- The executive directors will include the general manager of the hospital, a medical director, the senior nurse manager and a finance director. They will be full members of the board. The general manager will be appointed by the non-executive directors, and the other executive directors by the non-executive directors acting with the general manager.

3.5   NHS Hospital Trusts will be empowered by statute to employ staff; to enter into contracts both to provide services and to buy in services and supplies from others; and to raise income within the scope set by the Health and Medicines Act 1988.

3.6 An NHS Hospital Trust will earn its revenue from the services it provides. The main source of revenue will be from contracts with health authorities for the provision of services to their residents. Other contracts and revenue will come from GP practices with their own NHS budgets, private patients or their insurance companies, private hospitals, employers and, perhaps, other NHS Hospital Trusts. This form of funding will be a stimulus to better performance. There will be an opportunity to finance improved and expanded services because the money will flow to where the patients are going. Hospitals which prove more popular with GPs and patients will attract a larger share of NHS and other resources available for hospital services. A successful hospital will then be able to invest in providing still more and better services.

3.7 Contracts will need to spell out clearly what is required of each hospital in terms of the price, quality and nature of service to be provided. A hospital which fails to meet the terms of a contract will risk losing patients and revenue. The arrangements set out in chapter 4 will ensure that patients who are in need of urgent treatment are not turned away from a hospital simply because their treatment is not, or may not be, covered by a contract with that hospital. Of course there will be no question of patients who need urgent treatment being denied it.

3.8 Health authority funding will continue to be cash-limited, and this will place authorities under a strong incentive to secure value for money through their contracts. Performance-related contracts of employment will similarly provide strong incentives for hospital managers to improve the quantity and quality of the services on offer. Competition with other hospitals, where it is effective, should also constrain costs.

3.9 Each Health Department's Accounting Officer will have an overall responsibility for the stewardship of public funds by NHS Hospital Trusts. The Secretary of State will need specific powers for use in reserve to prevent any NHS Hospital Trust with anything near to a local monopoly of service provision from exploiting its position, for example by charging unreasonably high prices for its services.

FREEDOM AND RESPONSIBILITY

3.10 The Government proposes to give NHS Hospital Trusts a range of powers and freedoms which are not, and will not be, available to health authorities generally. Greater freedom will stimulate greater enterprise and commitment, which will in turn improve services for patients. NHS Hospital Trusts will be a novel part of a system of hospital care alongside health authority-managed and private sector hospitals, and will increase the range of choice available to patients and their GPs.

Employment of staff

3.11 The Government intends that NHS Hospital Trusts should be free to employ whatever and however many staff they consider necessary, except that junior doctors' posts will continue to need the approval of the relevant Royal College for training purposes. The Government sees it as particularly important that Trusts should employ their own consultants. Where consultants also work for other NHS hospitals or in the private sector, a Trust will need to employ them on a part-time basis consistent with their commitment to the Trust's hospital.

3.12 The Government also intends that NHS Hospital Trusts should be free to settle the pay and conditions of their staff, including doctors, nurses and others covered by national pay review bodies. Subject to their contractual obligations, NHS Hospital Trusts will be free either to continue to follow national pay agreements or to adopt partly or wholly different arrangements.

Ownership of assets

3.13 NHS Hospital Trusts will be constituted as public corporations. Each hospital's assets will be vested in its Trust, as follows:

- The Trust will be free to use the hospital's assets to provide health care, in accordance with stated purposes laid down by the Secretary of State when self-governing status is granted.

- The Trust will be free to dispose of its assets, subject only to a reserve power for the Secretary of State to intervene if a disposal would be against the public interest.

- When it is established, the Trust will be given an interest-bearing debt equal to the value of its initial assets. The effect of these and other arrangements for servicing capital will be consistent with that of the new capital charging system proposed for NHS hospitals generally in chapter 2.

- The Trust will be free to retain surpluses and to build up reserves with which to improve services and finance investment. It will also be free to manage any temporary deficits.

- The Trust's operations will be subject to independent audit by the Audit Commission in accordance with the proposals in chapter 2. The National Audit Office will have right of access to papers relating to the accounts and audit of NHS Hospital Trusts, and will be able to include them in their value for money studies.

- The hospital's assets will revert to the ownership of the Secretary of State if for any reason the Trust is wound up.

Borrowing powers

3.14 NHS Hospital Trusts will be free to borrow, either from the Government or from the private sector, subject to an overall annual financing limit. The Government will seek limited reserve powers for the Secretary of State to use if this freedom is being abused or if a Trust is getting into difficulties. The annual financing limit will be set each year by the Secretary of State following the Government's Public Expenditure Survey. Borrowing from the Government will be from funds voted by

Parliament. NHS Hospital Trusts will have to service their loans from their income, just as other NHS hospitals will be charged for their capital.

ACHIEVING SELF-GOVERNMENT

3.15 The Government will lay down a simple, flexible process for establishing an NHS Hospital Trust. It will be open to a variety of interests either to initiate the process or to respond to any initiative taken by the Secretary of State. These interests could include the District Health Authority (DHA), the hospital management team, a group of staff, or people from the local community who are active in the hospital's support.

3.16 The Government is not proposing a rigid definition of what a "hospital" should be for the purposes of self-government. For example, it will often be sensible for a hospital to retain its existing obligations to run a range of community-based services. Similarly, neighbouring hospitals may want to combine into a single management unit.

3.17 Hospitals will have to meet only a few essential conditions to achieve self-governing status. There will be two main criteria. First, management must have demonstrated the skills and capacity to run the hospital, including strong and effective leadership, sufficient financial and personnel management expertise and adequate information systems. Second, senior professional staff, especially consultants, must be involved in the management of the hospital. The Secretary of State will need to satisfy himself that self-governing status is not simply being sought as an alternative to an unpalatable but necessary closure. The NHS must not be obliged to retain hospitals which are redundant to its needs.

3.18 The Government will look to RHAs to play an active part in guiding and supporting hospitals which can be expected to meet these criteria and are interested in achieving self-government. In each case, the Secretary of State will need to satisfy himself at an early stage that there is a good prospect of being able to approve the creation of a new NHS Hospital

Trust. With the advice of the RHA, he will also need to identify a "shadow" chairman who can act for the hospital in preparing the ground.

3.19 NHS Hospital Trusts must also continue to provide essential core services to the local population, including accident and emergency facilities, where no alternative provision exists. RHAs will need to ensure that this is so when submitting and advising on a formal application to the Secretary of State. They will also need to ensure that the proposal to seek self-governing status is given adequate publicity locally.

3.20 The establishment of NHS Hospital Trusts will mean a substantial change in the responsibilities of the DHAs which were previously responsible for their management. As more and more proposals for establishing NHS Hospital Trusts come forward, RHAs will need to consider the viability of existing DHAs and the possibility of sensible mergers with neighbouring Districts. Larger Districts might eventually become candidates for mergers with Family Practitioner Committees.

IMPLEMENTATION

3.21 The Government believes that NHS Hospital Trusts have a major role to play in improving services to patients. It will therefore encourage as many major acute hospitals as possible to seek self-governing status. The Government's aim is to establish a substantial number of Trusts with effect from April 1991, in the wake of the necessary legislation. The experience gained will then inform the process of establishing more Trusts in later years. The Secretary of State will be issuing shortly a working paper which will set out in more detail the scope of self-governing status and proposals for implementing it, as a basis for discussion with interested parties.

3.22 The Government and RHAs will identify suitable early candidates for self-government and encourage them to seek and prepare for self-governing status. The aim will be to ensure that the hospitals concerned make productive use of the next two years by building up their capacity to run their own affairs effectively and by securing the maximum devolution of management responsibility from their DHAs. Self-government will then be - as it should be - a natural step forward from devolved management within the present structure.

CHAPTER 4:

FUNDING
HOSPITAL
SERVICES

INTRODUCTION

4.1 Hospital services must be funded in a way which encourages more choice and more value for money.

4.2 Chapters 2 and 3 of this White Paper set out the Government's proposals for delegating to hospitals themselves the main, operational responsibility for providing hospital services. At the moment, District Health Authorities (DHAs) provide those services and are funded to do so. The Government believes that the primary task of each DHA should be to secure the best and most cost-effective services it can for its patients, whether or not those services are provided by the District's own hospitals. This in turn implies that health authorities should be funded for the population they serve, and not for the services they provide.

4.3 Similarly, the Government believes that NHS hospitals should be free to offer their services to their own Districts and to other Districts in a way which enables them to attract the funds they need in line with the work they are asked to do. This means that hospitals should be funded more directly for the volume and quality of the services they provide. At present, a hospital which becomes more efficient and could treat more patients may be prevented from doing so by the budget imposed on it. Another, which is doing less work and operating at lower levels of efficiency, may still be funded at the same level. The Government is determined to change this by making it possible for the money available to treat patients to move more freely to the hospitals which offer patients the best service and the best value for money.

FUNDING HEALTH AUTHORITIES

The present system

4.4 Since 1977, money has been allocated to Regional Health Authorities (RHAs) on the basis of a formula which seeks to identify the health care needs of each Region's population. The formula is known as RAWP

(Resource Allocation Working Party). Each year, when making financial allocations to Regions, the Government decides how far actual allocations should move towards the target shares indicated by the formula. When the formula was introduced Regions were on average over eight per cent away from their RAWP targets, with a range from 11 per cent below to 15 per cent above. Now 11 of the 14 are within three per cent.

4.5 RHAs tend to vary in the extent to which they rely on the RAWP formula when allocating funds to Districts. In recent years, growth money has usually been allocated on the basis of planned service developments - for example, to enable a new hospital to open - rather than by a simple application of the formula.

4.6 The undesirable result of the present system is that there is no direct relationship between the amount of money a District is allocated and the number of patients its hospitals are treating. This is partly because the movement of patients across Regional boundaries is reflected only retrospectively in the formula, and because the resulting changes affect only target, not actual, allocations. Allocations to Districts also reflect historical patterns of service use and pay insufficient regard to varying levels of efficiency and performance. This confusing pattern is often the cause of local financial problems within a service whose total resources have been rising rapidly.

A new approach

4.7 The Government proposes to simplify and improve the arrangements for allocating funds to RHAs and DHAs. The underlying principles to be applied are the same in both cases. The Government recognises the need for a transitional period, which will be longer at District than at Regional level.

Allocations to RHAs

4.8 RHAs will be funded on a capitation basis, weighted to reflect the health and age distribution of the population, including the number of elderly people, and the relative costs of providing services. The Thames Regions will receive a slightly higher level of funding than the rest - some three per cent higher per head of population - to reflect the higher costs of and demands on services in the capital in particular. The Government aims to move to this new system over a two year period, starting in April 1990. There will be no separate "targets": the change to weighted capitation will bring actual allocations into line with a revised and simplified basis of funding.

4.9   From April 1990 allocations will be based on each Region's resident population. Regions will then pay each other directly, and therefore more quickly and in full, for the work they do for other Regions - so-called "cross-boundary flows". RHAs will be asked to agree the cost of these flows so that direct payment can start in 1990-91, initially by agreed cash limit adjustments until the Government has obtained the powers needed to enable health authorities to charge each other.

4.10   The arrangements described in paragraphs 4.8-4.9 will replace the use of the RAWP formula. The RAWP system has proved a useful method of producing a better distribution of resources nationally. But the Government has applied it over the years to such effect that the major differences have gone and it is no longer necessary. It would steadily become an academic exercise to try to get all Regions ever closer to complicated, ever-changing targets. The Government intends to move on from RAWP to a simpler and more predictable approach. Weighted capitation will be a fair and easy to understand system for providing health authorities with the means to buy the best possible service for patients in every part of the country.

Allocations to DHAs

4.11   At present Districts are funded mainly according to where hospitals happen to be located. In future, like Regions, they will be funded for their resident populations. Districts will pay directly for the services provided for their patients by hospitals in other Districts. The transition will take longer than at Regional level, and will depend on improving local information about population, the movement of patients and the costs of different treatments. The Government expects some DHAs to be in a position to pay each other directly from April 1991. Other authorities, drawing on the experience gained, will be expected to follow suit in the next year.

4.12 Even after adjusting for cross-boundary flows, there are significant differences between current District allocations and an approach based on weighted capitation. Residents in Districts with more hospital services tend to use them more than people with fewer local facilities. Differences in the quality of general practice or community-based services locally can also affect the use of hospital services and their cost. Districts will in due course be funded on broadly the same basis as Regions, but the Government recognises that to do so to the same timetable would in some cases involve sudden and substantial changes in the money available to buy services for each population. Such changes must be carefully managed over a transitional period as the overall level of resources grows. The Government will discuss with RHAs the detailed implementation of these proposals.

FUNDING HOSPITAL SERVICES

4.13 The present system of funding offers only limited incentives for hospitals to satisfy the needs and preferences of patients or to take on additional work by improving productivity. In future, each DHA's duty will be to buy the best service it can from its own hospitals, from other authorities' hospitals, from self-governing hospitals or from the private sector. Hospitals for their part will have to satisfy Districts that they are delivering the best and most efficient service. They will be free to offer their services to different health authorities.

4.14 The following paragraphs outline how this approach will work. The Secretary of State for Health will publish shortly a working paper which will set out the detail of how the changes required will be implemented, as a basis for discussion with interested parties.

"Core" services

4.15 There are many services to which patients need guaranteed local access. These "core" services can be divided into five broad categories:

- accident and emergency (A and E) departments;

- immediate admissions to hospital from an A and E department, including a significant proportion of general surgery;

- other immediate admissions, such as most general medicine and many hospital geriatric and psychiatric services;

- out-patient and other support services which are needed in support of the first three categories, either on site or immediately available;

- public health, community-based services and other hospital services which need to be provided on a local basis, either as a matter of policy - for example, services for elderly or mentally ill people - or on grounds of practicability - for example, district nursing and health visiting.

4.16 Where core services are provided by a hospital which continues to be managed directly by its DHA, they will be funded through a management budget. Management budgets will enable DHAs to set clear targets for the quantity and quality of the hospital's services, and to assess the hospital's performance against these targets. As better cost information becomes available, Districts will be able to refine and improve their target-setting and monitoring.

4.17 Alternatively, it will be possible for all or some of these core services to be bought by a District from an NHS Hospital Trust, or from a directly managed hospital in a neighbouring District, under an annually negotiated contract. Under this arrangement, hospitals will provide an agreed range of services, for a fixed payment, to all patients from the buying District who are referred or admitted.

4.18 The emergency services provided by a hospital will of course always be available immediately, without any question as to where the money is coming from. The Government will develop and implement its proposals in a way which ensures that the costs of emergency services and those requiring immediate admission to hospital can be met for every patient who needs them, irrespective of whether the patient is resident in a District which has a contract with the hospital.

Other services

4.19 Where patients and their GPs have time to choose when and where to seek hospital treatment, Districts will be able to buy services in a more flexible way. There are broadly three categories of such services:

- those which most Districts provide but for which patients may be prepared to travel if a better service is available elsewhere. These are mainly surgical operations, such as hernias and hip replacements, which make up the bulk of waiting lists.

- those not provided in every District, such as ear, nose and throat (ENT), ophthalmology and oral surgery;

- other services for which patients may wish to choose the location, for example some long-stay care for elderly people.

4.20 Most of these services will be provided under a contract which specifies a minimum and maximum number of cases to be treated. An initial payment would cover the minimum volume of work, with extra cases paid for as they arise, up to the specified maximum. The minimum payment assures the hospital of a contribution towards its fixed costs. This arrangement will apply to most in-patient and day case treatment within the services described in paragraph 4.19.

4.21 DHAs will want to keep a relatively small sum for buying services case by case, at a price quoted by a hospital. This opens up the scope for buying services at marginal cost as hospitals seek to use any spare capacity.

4.22 DHAs will be expected to use these new arrangements to offer more choice to patients. The range of choice available locally will depend in part on the accessibility of different hospitals. Districts will be free to buy from the private sector as well as from other Districts and from NHS Hospital Trusts.

4.23   Offering choice to patients means involving GPs far more in key decisions. When they place contracts, DHAs will need to take account of the existing referral patterns of GPs who have patients resident in their Districts. They will need to discuss with GPs the possibility of changing those patterns where they believe that better value for money can be obtained by doing so. GPs for their part will want to make sure that their views on the quality of care and shorter waiting times are reflected in a DHA's contracts. GPs who take part in the practice budget scheme set out in chapter 6 will be taking these decisions for themselves.

4.24   Under the present arrangements, hospitals are increasingly reluctant to accept referrals from GPs for patients who are not local residents, because there is no direct payment for cross-boundary flows. By enabling the patient's own DHA to pay for the services required, the Government's proposals will mean that hospitals accepting referrals from elsewhere will not have to do so at the expense of increasing waiting times for local patients. DHAs will need to allow for referrals by GPs to hospitals with whom no contracts have been placed, keeping some funds in reserve for this purpose.

4.25   For these new arrangements to work to best effect, GPs and their patients will need to be well informed about the choices on offer. The Government is putting further work in hand to help with this. It will improve information for GPs about their referral patterns. Information of this kind will be needed anyway for the practice budget scheme. It will be exploring how best to develop and publish indicators of hospital performance which cover the quality as well as the efficiency of the services provided. Subject to the forthcoming Monopolies and Mergers Commission report on restrictions on doctors' advertising, it will also discuss with the General Medical Council how to make it easier for hospital consultants to give GPs factual information about the services they offer.

4.26 The Government believes that these new funding arrangements will bring down waiting times for hospital treatment. They will move money to where the work is best done, and will make maximum waiting times an important feature of contracts and management budgets. DHAs, and GPs within the practice budget scheme, will seek to buy where waiting times are shortest, and hospitals will have a stronger incentive to reduce their waiting times in order to attract funds. In the meantime, the Government intends to build on the current waiting list initiative. The central waiting list fund will be targeted at Districts which show that they can use the extra money effectively.

Specialist services

4.27 Specialist services can be divided into two broad categories:

- so-called "supra-Regional" services. These are provided from a few, chosen national centres and are funded centrally. They include heart and liver transplants and neo-natal and infant cardiac surgery.

- Regional and "supra-District" services. These are designated by RHAs and may include cardiac surgery for adults, neo-natal intensive care and radiotherapy.

4.28 Most of these services will in future be bought by Districts for their resident patients from their basic allocations. Contracts will cover both direct referrals from the A and E department or GPs and referrals to a specialist consultant from another consultant. Some central funding will be necessary for the development of supra-Regional services, and RHAs may decide to adopt a similar approach to the funding of some Regional and supra-District services. The NHS Management Executive will discuss with RHAs the detailed application to specialist services of the new funding arrangements proposed.

Training and research

4.29 Most hospitals will incur costs which do not arise directly from the treatment of patients. The main examples are medical, nurse and other training; and research. Some of these costs are directly attributable to the training or research itself. Other costs arise from the impact of training or research needs on service costs.

4.30 The Government is firmly committed to maintaining the quality of medical education and research. It recognises the complexity and special needs of these areas. Health authorities involved in medical education incur additional costs which will continue to be reflected in the new funding arrangements through an improved "service increment for teaching" (SIFT). The Government has set up an inter-departmental Steering Group on Undergraduate Medical and Dental Education to examine the special problems of providing for medical education. The Group will develop its work, and make recommendations in the light of the proposals in this White Paper. The Government will discuss with RHAs and others concerned how best to ensure that other costs associated with training and research are also met without putting one hospital at an unfair disadvantage by comparison with another.

CHAPTER 5

INTRODUCTION

5.1 The NHS employs over 48,000 hospital doctors, of whom nearly 17,000 are consultants. The reforms proposed by the Government in this White Paper will make it easier for consultants and their colleagues to get on with the job of treating patients. The greater autonomy for hospitals proposed in chapters 2 and 3 will remove unnecessary central and Regional controls. The new funding arrangements set out in chapter 4 will steer resources to those consultants best able to provide a good quality service and to treat more patients. The expansion of the resource management initiative outlined in chapter 2 will give them budgetary and information systems more sensitively tuned to medical needs.

5.2 The decisions taken by consultants are critical to the way in which the money available for the NHS is used. It is therefore important to ensure that consultants are properly accountable for the consequences of these decisions. This chapter sets out the Government's proposals for striking a proper balance between two legitimate pressures, both of which are focused on patients' interests: the professional responsibilities and rewards of the individual consultant; and the responsibility of managers to ensure that the money available for hospitals buys the best possible service for patients.

MEDICAL AUDIT

5.3 A patient's primary concern, of course, is to be given a correct diagnosis and then to receive the best possible treatment. Within the next two years, the Government would like to see all hospital doctors taking part in what doctors themselves have come to call "medical audit" - a systematic, critical analysis of the quality of medical care, including the procedures used for diagnosis and treatment, the use of resources, and the resulting outcome for the patient.

5.4 Medical audit is essentially a professional matter. It is a means of ensuring, through peer review of medical practice, that the quality of medical work meets acceptable standards. It necessarily requires both specialised knowledge of current medical practice and access to adequate medical records.

5.5   Medical audit must be developed and implemented with care. Medicine is an inexact science, often lacking generally accepted measures of the benefits to patients from different techniques and services. Medical audit must not discourage doctors from taking on difficult but essential clinical work.

5.6   The Government welcomes the initiatives which the medical profession is already taking, both nationally and locally, to foster the development of medical audit, and aims to work with the profession to build on what has been achieved. For example, the Secretary of State for Health has asked the statutory Standing Medical Advisory Committee to consider and report on how the quality of medical care can best be improved by means of medical audit, and on the development of indicators of clinical outcome. The Government will also encourage all the Royal Colleges to make participation in medical audit a condition of a hospital unit being allowed to train junior doctors.

5.7   Management too has a responsibility to ensure that medical audit becomes firmly established, especially at local level. The Secretary of State will publish shortly a working paper which will set out the detail of how an effective framework for medical audit might be implemented, as a basis for discussion with interested parties. The Government's aim is to secure such a framework in all NHS hospitals, including self-governing hospitals, by April 1991.

5.8   The Government's approach is based firmly on the principle that the quality of medical work should be reviewed by a doctor's peers, whilst recognising also that management itself is responsible for ensuring that resources are used in the most effective way. The Government's main proposals are as follows:

•   Every consultant should participate in a form of medical audit agreed between management and the profession locally.

- The system should be medically led, with a local medical audit advisory committee chaired by a senior clinician.

- District management should be responsible for ensuring that an effective system of medical audit is in place, and also that the work of each medical team is reviewed at whatever regular, frequent intervals are agreed locally.

- Peer review findings in individual cases should be confidential, but the general results of medical audit should be available to management locally and the lessons learned published more widely.

- Management should be able to initiate an independent professional audit, for example where there is cause to question the quality or cost-effectiveness of a service. The possibility of independent doctors working jointly with the Audit Commission is discussed in paragraph 2.30.

5.9 The Government recognises that medical audit needs a significant investment of time by doctors themselves, and adequate support to ensure that the necessary information is available. The Government is confident that this investment will prove worthwhile by further improving the quality of service to NHS patients.

MANAGING THE CONSULTANT'S CONTRACT

5.10 Most hospital services are the responsibility of District Health Authorities (DHAs). But, with the exception of those working in Teaching Districts or for Special Health Authorities, consultants' contracts are held by Regional Health Authorities (RHAs). This has tended to cause confusion about the nature of a consultant's accountability to local management and the DHA. It has also tended to leave unclear what a District can and should expect of its consultants.

5.11 The Government believes that it is unacceptable for local management to have little authority or influence over those who are in practice responsible for committing most of the hospital service's resources. This does not mean moving consultants' contracts from RHAs to DHAs, which would cause unnecessary disruption. The Government proposes instead to ensure that each DHA acts as its RHA's agent in agreeing with consultants the scope and arrangement of their NHS duties in each hospital. NHS Hospital Trusts will employ their own consultants, as proposed in chapter 3.

Job descriptions

5.12 The key to the local management of consultants' contracts is that every consultant should have a fuller job description than is commonly the case at present. This will need to cover their responsibility for the quality of their work, their use of resources, the extent of the services they provide for NHS patients and the time they devote to the NHS. These job descriptions, which will be reviewable annually, will be an essential tool for managing all consultants' contracts. They will need to be sufficiently detailed, for example as to the number of outpatient clinics which a consultant is expected to hold, to enable District management to monitor whether consultants are fulfilling their contractual obligations.

5.13 DHAs will be asked to agree a job description along these lines with each of their consultants. They will need to do so in a way which preserves both the freedom of consultants to take clinical decisions within the boundaries of accepted professional standards and their 24-hour responsibility for their patients. The Government will discuss with management and the medical profession nationally how best to implement this, including a suitable national framework for consultants' job descriptions.

Appointments

5.14 There is currently no provision for District management to take a full and formal part in the appointment of a consultant. Consultant appointments are recommended by mainly professional Advisory Appointment Committees, whose primary consideration is the professional suitability of the candidate. The Government will seek to amend the Appointment of Consultants Regulations to enable District General Managers to take part directly in the appointments procedure. Professional suitability will and should remain essential, but the general manager's presence will help the Committee to take into account a candidate's willingness and ability to meet the requirements of the post for the management of resources and the development of services.

Disciplinary procedures

5.15 The Government intends to complement these changes by improving the present disciplinary procedures for consultants. These procedures are at present cumbersome and inflexible. They have recently been reviewed by a Joint Working Party of the Health Departments and the profession, established by the Government in 1987. The Working Party has made a number of valuable recommendations. The Government will now open negotiations with the profession on the basis of the Working Party's report.

5.16 The Government sets particular store by two of the changes which the Working Party suggests. The first is the introduction of new, local procedures for dealing with circumstances which warrant disciplinary action short of dismissal. The second concerns the right of a consultant dismissed by his employer to appeal to the Secretary of State against his dismissal. This can be a time-consuming and costly process, the prospect of which may deter management from embarking on dismissal proceedings in the first place. The Government therefore welcomes the Working Party's proposal for a timetable which should lead to concluding an appeal within not more than nine months of the dismissal.

REFORM OF DISTINCTION AWARDS

5.17 Some 35 per cent of consultants currently receive of a distinction award. This takes the form of a superannuable increase in salary at one of four levels. There are currently some 3,900 'C' awards (£6,260), 1700 'B' awards (£14,200), 700 'A' awards (£24,850) and nearly 200 'A+' awards (£33,720) in Great Britain. Distinction awards are intended to reward clinical excellence, and are payable until retirement. The normal pattern is for progression through the levels of awards. New and increased awards are given on the advice of an independent professional committee.

5.18 The distinction awards scheme was introduced in 1948, and has remained substantially unchanged since then. In their 1988 report (Cm 358), the Review Body on Doctors' and Dentists' Remuneration suggested that expenditure on the scheme should result as far as possible in a benefit to the NHS, as well as rewarding doctors for their individual efforts. The Government agrees. It believes that the nature and administration of the scheme should now be changed, with two main objectives in view: to reflect the wider responsibilities of consultants for the effective use of resources, as well as the clinical merit of their work; and to ensure that the scheme offers consultants stronger incentives to maintain and improve their contribution to local services.

5.19 The Government proposes to open discussions with the medical profession nationally with the following changes in mind:

• to modify the criteria for 'C' awards, so that in future consultants must demonstrate not only their clinical skills but also a commitment to the management and development of the service. There will be limited exceptions, to meet the circumstances of consultants whose jobs include only a small management content.

• to restrict progression to the remaining three levels of awards to those consultants who have earned 'C' awards.

• to change the composition of the regional committees which nominate candidates for 'C' awards. In future, each committee will be chaired by the RHA Chairman and will include senior managers as well as clinicians.

- to change the composition of the national Advisory Committee on Distinction Awards, to provide for a stronger management influence on the choice of award holders.

- to make new or increased awards reviewable every five years.

- to make new or increased awards pensionable only if a consultant continues working in the NHS for at least three years.   The Government believes that this will meet the criticism made by the Review Body that awards given to those approaching retirement, with the additional pension benefits entailed, can hardly be said to be in the best interests of the Service.

ADDITIONAL CONSULTANTS

5.20   The Government believes that faster progress in reducing waiting times for treatment and in improving the quality of services for NHS patients can be made by the creation of more consultant posts. This would also help to improve the career prospects, and to reduce the working hours, of junior doctors. The Government therefore proposes to introduce a scheme under which 100 additional, permanent consultant posts can be created over the next three years. The cost of these posts will be met over and above the cost of the two per cent annual expansion in consultant numbers already planned. The scheme will concentrate on increasing the number of consultants in those acute specialties which currently have the longest waiting times for treatment.

PART THREE: GENERAL PRACTICE

- The service offered by the family GP is one of the greatest strengths of the NHS. On average, people consult their GP between four and five times a year. For most it is their first port of call if they are feeling unwell. The vast majority of medical care is provided outside hospitals.

- Of those who go into hospital some may go or be taken there direct, for example in an emergency. More usually, people who need hospital services - consultation with a specialist, diagnostic tests, or even immediate admission as an in-patient - are referred by their GP. The GP is each patient's key adviser. He or she is best qualified to advise on whether or not someone needs to go to hospital, on which hospitals offer the best service, and on who are the best specialists to consult. The GP - acting on behalf of patients - is the gatekeeper to the NHS as a whole.

- The GP's advice will therefore be crucial if patients are tobenefit fully from the reformed hospital service described in Part Two of this White Paper. Part Three addresses more directly the central role of the GP. Chapter 6 outlines a scheme for giving larger GP practices the money with which they can buy directly a defined range of the services they and their patients want. Chapter 7 sets out proposals for securing still better value for money from the family doctor service itself.

GP
PRACTICE
BUDGETS

INTRODUCTION

6.1   The relationships which GPs have with both patients and hospitals make them uniquely placed to improve patients' choice of good quality services. There are three main obstacles to further progress:

  • Hospitals and their consultants need a stronger incentive to look on GPs as people whose confidence they must gain if patients are to be referred to them.

  • For the reasons set out in chapter 4, a GP who refers a patient to another District's hospital can cause financial problems for the hospital if it accepts the referral. As a result, waiting lists may grow and waiting times lengthen.

  • GPs themselves lack incentives to offer their patients a choice of hospital.

6.2   To help tackle these problems in a way which builds on the strong foundations of the family doctor service, the Government will introduce a new scheme for enabling money to flow with the patient from the GP practice itself. The practices and hospitals which attract the most custom will receive the most money. Both GPs and hospitals will have a real incentive to put patients first. The Government believes that this reform will deliver better care for patients, shorter waiting times, and better value for money.

6.3   The Government also believes that the scheme will be attractive to the many GPs who are keen to improve the services they offer. It will enable the practices which take part to play a more important role in the way in which NHS money is used to provide services for their patients. It will give them scope to plough back savings into their practices. General practice will become a still more satisfying job.

How practice budgets will work

6.4 At the start of the new scheme, GP practices with lists of at least 11,000 patients (see paragraph 6.7) will be free to apply for their own NHS budgets for a defined range of hospital services.They will be able to obtain these services from either NHS or private sector hospitals. The size of each practice's budget will depend primarily on the number of patients on the practice's list. There will be three categories of hospital services within the scheme:

- out-patient services, including associated diagnostic and treatment costs. With the exception of expensive out-patient treatment which has to be provided on a hospital site - radiotherapy, for example - continuing out-patient treatment will be included.

- a defined group of in-patient and day case treatments, such as hip replacements and cataract removals, for which there may be some choice over the time and place of treatment. The inclusion of this category will make it easier for GPs to offer shorter waiting times to patients who are willing to travel, and will enable them to provide the hospitals concerned with NHS funds to pay for the treatment. The Government will consult on the precise list of treatments to be covered.

- diagnostic tests, such as X-ray examinations and pathology tests, which are undertaken by hospitals at the direct request of GPs.

6.5 In addition, the Government intends the scheme to cover three important aspects of the services provided by GPs themselves:

- the 70 per cent of practice team staff costs which is directly reimbursed to GP practices at present and which will be cash-limited under the Health and Medicines Act 1988. The inclusion of staff costs within the budget will encourage practices to consider whether, for example, to employ more nursing or other staff and make less use of out-patient services.

- improvements to practice premises. The assistance available to GPs in improvement grants and under the cost rent scheme will also be cash-limited under the 1988 Act and will be included.

- prescribing costs. Chapter 7 sets out the Government's proposals for setting indicative drug budgets for GPs generally. GPs within the practice budgets scheme will have their own drug budgets.

6.6 Participation in the practice budget scheme will be voluntary, and practices which have joined the scheme will be free to leave it again if they wish, after giving due notice.

6.7 Although the different elements within a practice budget will be determined in different ways - as outlined in paragraph 6.9 below - the result will be a single budget. Budgets will need to be large enough to cope with fluctuations in demand. The Government proposes that at the outset of the scheme, participation should be limited to practices with lists of at least 11,000 patients, which is twice the national average. This should ensure that most participating practices will have annual budgets of some £600-700,000. On this basis over 1,000 practices will be eligible in the UK, which is nine per cent of all practices covering between them about a quarter of the population. The Government will consider relaxing the 11,000 patient minimum if experience shows that budgets for practices of this size are more than large enough to allow for the necessary flexibility.

Determination of budgets

6.8 GP practices within the scheme will receive their budgets direct from the relevant Regional Health Authority (RHA). The Family Practitioner Committee (FPC) will continue to hold the GPs' contracts and be responsible for monitoring expenditure against the budget.

6.9 The size of each practice's budget will be settled by the RHA with the practice within national guidelines designed to ensure fairness and consistency. Each budget will be determined along broadly the following lines:

- The hospital services element will be funded from the revenue allocation which the RHA itself receives from the Government for hospital and community health services. Each practice's share will be based on the number of patients on its list, weighted for the same population characteristics as are proposed in chapter 4 for allocations to Districts. There are social and other local features which affect the use of hospital services, and these too will be reflected in the budget. The amount given to the practice will be deducted from the relevant District allocations.

- The element of the budget which is attributable to practice staff and premises improvements will be based initially on the existing amounts which the FPC provides to the practice for these purposes, together with a proportional share of any additional cash allocated to the FPC in future.

- The prescribing costs element will be found from within the overall drug budget allocated to the RHA in accordance with the proposals set out in chapter 7.

6.10 The Secretary of State will publish shortly a working paper which will set out the detail of how these and other proposals described in this chapter will be implemented, as a basis for discussion with interested parties.

THE MANAGEMENT OF PRACTICE BUDGETS

Obtaining hospital services

6.11 Where costs are to some extent under the direct control of the practice itself, as with practice staff and premises improvements, GPs should have relatively little difficulty in keeping within budget. But the costs incurred by hospitals in treating each patient referred by the GP are not within the GP's own control. It is essential that practices are able to manage their total expenditure, without denying services to their patients. It is also important that they do so in a way which enables them to negotiate the best deals they can.

6.12 To this end, practices within the scheme will need to make full use of the range of methods of funding hospital services described in chapter 4. To cover initial referrals for out-patient appointments, for example, a practice may wish to negotiate fixed-price contracts for each specialty with particular hospitals. The hospital would then provide an agreed range of out-patient services to patients referred from the practice. In this way any patient who needed the urgent advice of a specialist would be able to get it. Practices will want to hold some money back, to keep open the possibility of obtaining services at marginal cost where hospitals have spare capacity to offer in the course of the year. GPs themselves will be responsible for deciding the best mix of budgeting and contractual arrangements for their practices, in the light of the working paper on contracts referred to in chapter 4. The Government will ensure that ideas and experience are widely disseminated.

Scope for flexibility

6.13 Practices within the scheme will be well placed to generate savings within their budgets. The Government intends that they should be able to spend any such savings to plough money back into improving their practices as they judge best and offering more and better services to their patients.

6.14 Urgent treatment must always be available to patients in all circumstances. If for good clinical reasons a practice finds itself overspending its budget in any year, the Government will allow it to overspend by up to 5 per cent in that year. The RHA will provide for that overspend within its overall cash limit. Any overspending will be recouped in the following year. If a practice overspends in excess of 5 per cent, or persistently overspends at a lower level, the FPC will initiate a thorough audit, including a review by other doctors of any medical judgements which seem to be causing budgetary problems. An overspend in excess of 5 per cent for two years in succession may result in a practice losing the right to hold its own budget.

Management costs

6.15 Each practice's budget will include a fee to cover the management and other costs, including start-up costs, of participating in the scheme.

IMPLEMENTATION

6.16 The Government's aim is to encourage a substantial number of GP practices to apply to manage their own budgets with effect from April 1991, with more practices joining the scheme in subsequent years. In the meantime, the Government will seek the necessary powers to enable GP practices to buy hospital services in the ways proposed. It will also encourage and invest in the development of the information systems which will be needed to support the calculation of budgets, the pricing and costing of hospital services to GPs, and the monitoring of prescribing costs.

6.17 The Government will look to RHAs and FPCs to give a positive lead in guiding and supporting GP practices which are interested in joining the scheme. The decision on any application will rest with the relevant RHA in each case, subject to a right of appeal to the Secretary of State. In reaching its decision the RHA will need to consider two main factors: first, the ability of the practice to manage its budget effectively, for example its practice management capacity, its technology and its access to hospital information; and, second, the GPs' commitment to, and policies for, taking individual decisions within a collective budget.

CHAPTER 7:

MANAGING THE FAMILY PRACTITIONER SERVICES

| INTRODUCTION |

7.1   The reforms of the hospital and community health services set out in this White Paper make it possible and necessary to build further on the policies already set out in the Government's White Paper on primary health care, "Promoting Better Health" (Cm 249). General practice will play an even greater role in assisting patient choice and directing resources to match patient needs throughout the whole Health Service as a result of the Government's new policies. The Government believes that, in order to play this key role to the full, general practice will need strengthening in four areas: patient choice; medical audit; prescribing costs; and management. In each case the Government's proposals complement those in the rest of this White Paper by aiming to improve services for patients, both directly and through achieving better value for money.

| PATIENT CHOICE |

7.2   In "Promoting Better Health", the Government described a range of measures it intended to introduce to put the patient first. A better informed public, a remuneration system geared to patient choice, and better value for money, were seen as key means to this end. This White Paper provides an opportunity for the Government to develop further some key objectives.

Capitation fees

7.3   At present, capitation fees form on average 46 per cent of a GP's income. "Promoting Better Health" stated the Government's intention to raise this proportion. The Government remains of the view that GPs will have a stronger incentive to satisfy their patients if a greater proportion of their income is attributable to the number of patients on their lists. The Government intends, therefore, to raise the average remuneration accounted for by capitation fees from 46 per cent to at least 60 per cent, as soon as possible. This will still allow scope for targeted incentive payments, for example for childhood immunisation or cervical cancer screening, and special arrangements for practices in deprived inner cities and thinly populated rural areas. Basic practice allowance will form a reduced proportion of remuneration, and its level will vary according to the location of the practice; in some cases it will be reduced to zero.

Choosing a doctor

7.4   The Government also remains determined that patients must be able to exercise a real choice between GPs. "Promoting Better Health" outlined two particularly important changes to this end.

7.5   The first change is to give patients the opportunity to make a better informed choice. GP practices will be encouraged to produce and distribute information about the services they offer. The Government believes that the advertising of services offered by practices should become the norm, subject only to safeguards necessary to protect the quality of professional services available.

7.6   The second key change is to enable patients to register with a new doctor without having to go through the present restrictive procedure, which requires them first to approach their existing doctor and Family Practitioner Committee (FPC). Patients should be quite free to choose and change their doctor without any hindrance at all, and the Government will bring forward the necessary amending Regulations as soon as possible.

Better information for doctors

7.7   If they are to make the best use of resources and services on behalf of their patients, family doctors need good information on, for example, waiting times, hospital referrals and prescribing patterns. Many doctors' practices are already computerised, but there is scope for considerable further development to enhance the service which doctors can offer their patients.

7.8   In "Promoting Better Health", the Government announced its intention to encourage the continued development of information and communication technology and computerisation in primary care. The Government will make available additional resources for the development of computer systems in general practice and for health authorities and FPCs to develop systems which improve the flow of information to GPs. The Government will discuss its proposals for development in this field with all interested parties.

MEDICAL AUDIT

7.9 As with the hospital service, the Government intends to work with the medical profession nationally to establish a system of medical audit in general practice. A good deal is already being achieved by the profession itself, for example through the Royal College of General Practitioners' "Quality Initiative". The Government's aim will be to build on these foundations.

7.10 The organisation of medical audit will be less straightforward than in hospitals. Care is delivered in more places; periods of treatment are less well defined; medical records are usually less detailed. But the Government is confident that these are difficulties which can be overcome. It believes that the following key features will be generally applicable to medical audit in general practice:

- medical audit locally should be based both on peer review and on self-audit by GPs and GP practices;

- local practice and procedures should be led, supported and encouraged by a medical audit advisory committee established by each FPC;

- each FPC, in consultation with its GPs, should set up a small unit of doctors and other staff to support and monitor the medical audit procedures of its practices;

- the local medical audit advisory committee should guide the work of the medical audit unit and, where necessary, help to arrange an external peer review of a GP or GP practice;

• FPCs should have access to the general results of medical audits of GPs.

7.11 The Government will consult the profession and FPC interests fully on the detailed implementation of medical audit in general practice. The Government believes that, once a satisfactory system has been developed, all GPs should be required by their contracts to take part.

PRESCRIBING COSTS

The present position

7.12 The drugs bill is the largest single element - more than a third - of total expenditure on the family practitioner services (FPS). The cost of medicines accounted for £1.9 billion in 1987-88, more than the cost of the doctors who wrote the prescriptions. Expenditure on medicines has grown on average by four per cent a year above the rate of inflation over the past five years.

7.13 There are wide differences in drug costs from one part of the UK to another, varying from £26 per head of population in one locality to £48 in another. To some extent these variations result from differences in population structure and morbidity. But they also reflect varying attitudes to prescribing by doctors who have no direct interest in the cost of the drugs which they prescribe.

7.14 Following the introduction of the Selected List - which saved £75 million in the drugs bill in its first year of operation, to the benefit of the rest of the NHS - the Government invited the medical profession to take part in voluntary measures to improve prescribing practices. The major result of this was the introduction of a new prescribing information system - known as "PACT" - which provides good quality data on doctors' prescribing patterns and how they compare with others.

Indicative drug budgets

7.15 The Government now proposes to build on these arrangements through a system of indicative drug budgets for GPs. The objective of this scheme is to place downward pressure on expenditure on drugs, particularly in those practices with the highest expenditure, but without in any way preventing people getting the medicines they need. In this way prescribing can be improved and wasteful expenditure avoided, for the benefit of the NHS as a whole.

7.16 Each year the provision made for FPS drug costs in the Parliamentary Estimates will be divided into separate firm budgets among the 14 health Regions, and RHAs will set drug budgets for each FPC on the basis of reasonable assumptions about prescribing costs in the FPC's area. FPCs will then set indicative budgets for each practice in discussion with the GPs themselves, taking into account both existing prescribing costs and the average for practices in similar circumstances. In determining the total amount available for drug spending, the Government will provide for the medicines which people need, to be supplied at reasonable prices, and will allow for the introduction of new drugs. The amount determined for a particular year may subsequently need to be revised as a result, for example, of severe cold weather or an influenza epidemic, but otherwise RHAs and FPCs will be expected to work to the budget they have been given.

7.17 FPCs will need to monitor spending during the year and discuss with any practice which appears likely to exceed its indicative budget the reasons for this - which may of course be entirely acceptable - and any steps it should take to curb spending. RHAs in turn will monitor the performance of FPCs. Any overspending will be taken into account when the following year's overall regional allocations are determined. The PACT information will be used initially to monitor spending against budgets, but because this is derived from prescriptions sent by pharmacists for pricing and payment there will inevitably be delay in providing doctors with the necessary information on this basis. An improved information system will therefore be needed before the new scheme can operate fully. Subject to further consideration of the details of the scheme, the Government will aim to introduce it with effect from April 1991. In the meantime action to encourage more economical prescribing, through the dissemination of information and monitoring of GPs, will continue.

The operation of the scheme

7.18 The Secretary of State for Health will publish shortly a working paper which will set out the detail of how the scheme will be implemented, for discussion with interested parties. The paper will cover:

- the factors to be taken into account and the weight to be attached to each of them in setting indicative budgets for practices;

- how best to provide up-to-date information about doctors' prescribing;

- the place of local formularies (locally agreed lists of drugs which would normally be prescribed in the majority of cases) by which FPCs and District Health Authorities (DHAs) can establish rational prescribing policies covering both the FPS and the hospital and community health services in the area.

7.19 Where a GP practice exceeds its indicative budget, the FPC's first recourse will be to offer advice and, where necessary, to bring a process of peer review to bear on the GPs' prescribing practices. The Government will also seek powers to enable FPCs to impose financial penalties on GPs who persistently refuse to curb excessive prescribing. The working paper referred to in paragraph 7.18 will cover the detailed application of these sanctions.

7.20 As part of the drug budget scheme, it will be possible for an FPC to agree with its GPs that they should aim for expenditure lower than the drug budget which the RHA had given to the FPC. In these cases, where the target is achieved, half the saving will be retained by the FPC and spent on schemes of improvement in primary health care in their areas as agreed with their GPs. For the first time, this will give the medical profession a positive incentive, linked to their interest in improving primary health care, to encourage cost-effective and prudent prescribing.

7.21 In "Promoting Better Health", the Government set out its intentions to strengthen the management of the FPS. This becomes even more important as a result of the additional tasks which those responsible for the FPS will acquire under the proposals in this White Paper. The rest of this chapter sets out the Government's further plans for strengthening the management of the FPS.

GP numbers

7.22 It is the Government's responsibility to ensure that there is adequate access to family doctors across the country; that opportunities exist for good doctors to enter general practice; and that there is a sensible, overall balance between the numbers of doctors in hospitals on the one hand and in general practice on the other. The Government proposes to take two further steps to enable it better to control the total cost of the service while ensuring that sufficient opportunities remain in general practice. First, it will seek reserve powers to control, if necessary, the number of GPs entering into contract with the NHS. Second, it will seek in due course to reduce from 70 to 65 the retirement age for GPs which has been introduced through the Health and Medicines Act 1988.

Composition of FPCs

7.23 FPCs normally consist of 15 members from the contractor professions and 15 lay members, plus a chairman. The chairman may be either professional or lay. All the members are appointed by the Secretary of State. The 15 professional members are drawn from nominations made by the professions' local representatives. Four of the lay members are drawn from DHA nominees, and a further four from local authority nominees.

7.24 The Government does not believe that a committee with 30 members can lead the management of the FPS as effectively as the changes now envisaged will require. Further, it is difficult for the management of contracts with practitioners to be the responsibility of bodies on which half the members are nominated by representatives of the practitioners whose contracts are to be managed. The Government will therefore seek powers to change the composition of FPCs so that their membership consists of:

- 11 members in total, including a chairman appointed by the Secretary of State;

- four professional members - a doctor in general practice, a dentist, a community pharmacist and a nurse with experience of community care - all appointed by the RHA and serving in a personal, not a representative, capacity;

- five lay members, appointed by the RHA and chosen for their experience and personal qualities;

- a chief executive, appointed by the chairman and lay members.

The Government will ensure that the new lay membership will preserve a measure of continuity with FPCs as currently constituted.

7.25 The currently extensive FPC sub-committee structure will be considerably slimmed down. The working paper referred to in paragraph 7.18 will set out the basis on which FPCs will be able to co-opt members to the remaining sub-committees.

7.26 The local committees representing the practitioner professions will continue to have an important role to play in the development of services, and FPCs will consult them in carrying out their functions.

Executive management

7.27 The Government proposes to create new chief executive posts in all FPCs, to be filled by open competition. The salaries for these new posts will be set significantly above those of the present FPC administrators, so as to be attractive to good quality managers from both inside and outside the NHS. FPCs will also need to strengthen their management and administration generally. The main task of the new chief executives will be to supply the drive needed to manage change, working closely with the contractor professions themselves.

Accountability of FPCs

7.28   Since the 1985 reorganisation, the Government has achieved some substantial improvements in the performance of FPCs. A good deal has been done in setting objectives for the FPS and in carrying out performance reviews to assess the progress made by FPCs in achieving those objectives. It has been possible to introduce and complete a computerisation programme, so that every FPC can now not only do its work more efficiently but can also call and re-call patients for essential preventive services such as cervical cytology.

7.29   The Government now intends to make FPCs accountable to RHAs, as are DHAs. This change will bring responsibility for primary health care and hospital services together at a strategic level. It will then be easier to plan and monitor effectively comprehensive policy initiatives spanning both services, for example in the field of health promotion and disease prevention. It is no longer necessary for the Department to be so directly involved in local management nor for it to hold directly accountable as many as 90 different bodies.

PART FOUR: OTHER ISSUES

CHAPTER 8 :

HEALTH AUTHORITY MEMBERSHIP

INTRODUCTION

8.1 Today's Health Service is a complex, multi-billion pound enterprise. Demand is continually increasing while resources are inevitably limited. The Government recognises the demands that this places on health authority chairmen and members and greatly appreciates their work.

8.2 Chairmen and members of health authorities will continue to have a vital role in the management of the Service and will need to spearhead the changes that the Government is proposing in this White Paper. Because so much management responsibility is now to be delegated to local level, the Government has decided that the membership of authorities should reflect this new role.

COMPOSITION OF HEALTH AUTHORITIES

8.3 Regional and District Health Authorities (RHAs and DHAs) currently comprise a chairman and between 16 and 19 members. The chairmen and members of RHAs are appointed by the Secretary of State. The chairmen of DHAs are also appointed by the Secretary of State, and most of the members are appointed by the relevant RHA. The RHA is required to consult various interests, and must appoint a representative of the appropriate university. Between four and six of the members of DHAs are directly appointed by relevant local authorities.

8.4 At District level, the arrangements for appointing members reflect a long-standing lack of clarity about the role of health authorities. At present, they are neither truly representative nor management bodies. Many members, such as those appointed directly by local authorities or on the advice of trades unions and professional bodies, usually regard themselves as representatives. But as a body they are often confronted by the need to take detailed decisions on key management issues. And the actual managers themselves are not members of the authority.

8.5 The Government believes that authorities based on this confusion of roles would not be equipped to handle the complex managerial and contractual issues that the new system of matching resources to performance will demand. The members needed to work in the new system should be appointed on the strength of the skills and experience they can bring to an authority's work. If health authorities are to discharge their new responsibilities in a business-like way, they need to be smaller and to bring together executive and non-executive members to provide a single focus for effective decision-making.

8.6 The Government therefore proposes that, with effect from the earliest possible date following the necessary legislation:

- RHAs and DHAs will be reduced from their present 16-19 members to five non-executive and up to five executive members, plus a non-executive chairman.

- The Secretary of State will be responsible for appointing the chairmen and non-executive members of RHAs and the chairmen of DHAs.

- RHAs will be responsible for appointing the non-executive members of DHAs.

- Non-executive members will be appointed solely on the basis of the skills and experience they can bring to the authority.

- The executive members will include the general manager and the finance director. The general manager will be appointed by the non-executive members, and the other executive members by the non-executive members acting with the general manager.

- Local authorities will no longer have a right to appoint members to DHAs.

- Teaching Districts will continue to include someone drawn from the medical school.

- RHAs will include a Family Practitioner Committee (FPC) chairman.

8.7   The interests of the local community will continue to be represented by Community Health Councils , which act as a channel for consumer views to health authorities and FPCs.

CHAPTER 9

SCOPE OF THE INDEPENDENT HEALTH SECTOR

9.1 Since 1948 the Health Service has been complemented by an independent health sector made up of a broad spectrum of private, voluntary and charitable bodies. The independent sector has complemented the Health Service not only in areas such as elective surgery where public provision is universal, but also in areas where NHS coverage is limited. These range from hospices, nursing and convalescent homes to fitness training, screening and chiropody. Its contribution to health care in the UK is now very substantial:

- 5.34 million people, or nine per cent of the population of the UK, are covered by private insurance;

- its acute hospitals have six per cent of acute beds and treat over 510,000 in-patients and day cases a year;

- it carries out 17 per cent of all elective surgery in England, including 28 per cent of all hip replacements and 19 per cent of all coronary artery by-pass grafts;

- it provides some 70 per cent of all hospice beds;

- there are some 78,000 beds in nursing homes, accounting for virtually all nursing home provision.

9.2 The advantages brought by the independent sector are that it:

- increases the range of options available to patients and their GPs;

- contributes, and could contribute more, to the cost-effective treatment of NHS patients, increasing the options available to NHS management as well as to individual patients;

- responds flexibly and rapidly to patients' needs.

These advantages can be developed to the benefit of all patients. Just as the private sector has no monopoly of efficiency or in quality of hotel services, so public provision has no monopoly of caring or quality of clinical treatment.

9.3   More and more people are looking to the private health sector for diagnosis and treatment. Between 1981 and 1986, the number of in-patients treated in independent hospitals in England and Wales grew by nearly a half to over 400,000. During the same period the number of day cases doubled to 100,000.

9.4   The Government welcomes this increase, not only because it relieves pressure on the NHS but also because it increases the opportunities for the NHS and the independent sector to learn from each other, to support each other and to buy and sell services to each other. The Government's reforms will open up further opportunities for the two sectors to work together for their mutual benefit.

9.5   There is already a growing partnership between the NHS and the independent health sector. In 1986, contractual arrangements between the NHS and the independent sector led to over 26,000 in-patient treatments at a cost of some £45 million. Many of these are long-term contracts. As part of the Government's drive to reduce hospital waiting lists, many health authorities have entered short-term contracts with private hospitals specifically to treat waiting list cases.

9.6   The Government believes that there is considerable scope for building on these initiatives. Under the proposals set out in chapter 6, GPs and their patients will be able to use NHS funds to pay for treatment in the private sector for certain conditions if this offers better quality or better value for money than buying NHS services. Similarly, health authorities carrying out their new role of purchasers rather than providers of care will buy in services from the private sector if it offers a better deal than is available from NHS hospitals.

9.7   If health authorities are to make the best use of private sector facilities, they will need to be satisfied that the standard of medical care being offered is comparable to the standards expected within the Health Service.

CHOOSING INDEPENDENT HEALTH CARE

9.8   A key factor in the development of the private sector has been the spread of private medical insurance. The number of people insured has grown significantly in the past few years: the biggest single element has been the increase in the provision of medical insurance cover by companies for their employees. But in most cases this cover stops when an individual retires. As a result, people are faced with deciding whether to take out cover as individuals at a time when their income has fallen and when medical insurance premiums rise.

9.9   To help meet this problem, and to encourage both the provision of medical insurance for older people and its take-up, the Government has decided to introduce legislation to give income tax relief from April 1990 on premiums for those aged 60 and over, whether paid by them or, for example, by their families on their behalf.

COMPETITIVE TENDERING

9.10 The Government launched a competitive tendering initiative in 1983 for domestic cleaning, catering and laundry services. Five years later that initiative has generated savings on these services approaching £120 million a year across the UK - some 17 per cent of previous costs. This is not simply a reflection of efficiency in the private sector since some 85 per cent of contracts were won in-house, despite the keen competition. Competition has not only produced substantial savings. It has also led to clearer performance criteria, improved productivity, innovative ideas and techniques, and better management.

9.11 The range of support services which NHS management at local level is now testing or planning to test through competitive tender is widening all the time. The total value of NHS services now subject to regular tendering is well in excess of £1 billion a year. Examples include portering, estate services, linen rental, computer services, security, distribution, design, and sometimes individual package contracts which cover a wide range of support services on the same site.

9.12 The Government believes that there is scope for much wider use of competitive tendering, beyond the non-clinical support services which have formed the bulk of tendering so far. This can extend as far as the wholesale "buying in" of treatments for patients from private sector hospitals and clinics, as has proved effective under the Government's waiting list initiative. But competitive tendering should not be just a "top down" exercise. The Government's objectives of delegating decision-making to the operational level and introducing more choice into the provision of services will greatly increase the opportunities for managers to buy in services from the private sector where this will improve the services to patients. Health authorities and their managers will be expected to consider such opportunities as an option in carrying out their new role.

JOINT VENTURES

9.13 There is a range of schemes open to health authorities which involve co-operation with the private sector and, by allowing the shared use of expensive facilities, can spread the costs to the benefit of each partner. These include:

• sharing the construction of hospital facilities with costs apportioned according to the use each sector plans to make of them. These schemes create opportunities for trading between the two sectors, with the private sector selling capacity to the NHS and the NHS selling diagnostic services, for example, to the private sector.

- leasing NHS land, buildings or other facilities to the private sector, which develops and runs health or other facilities on an NHS hospital site. The lease can be on conventional repayment terms, or can enable the NHS as landlord to share some of the profits generated by the lessee.

- leasing part of a hospital site to a housing association to provide low-cost accommodation for NHS staff. The housing association can either build afresh or refurbish existing accommodation.

9.14 In addition, the imaginative use of private sector skills - and sometimes financing - can result in more cost-effective and quicker development of new and existing services. For example, the Government intends that, subject to the approval of individual schemes, it will be possible for a private developer to provide a new hospital for a District Health Authority (DHA) on a green-field site. In effect, the developer is providing bridging finance for the DHA between the construction costs and the land sales receipts. The objective would be a hospital with lower running costs, built more quickly.

9.15 The professional advisers referred to in paragraph 2.26 will be available to advise authorities on the most effective use of under-used assets or development potential.

9.16 Taken together, the Government believes that schemes of this kind hold major potential benefits for each partner. The Government expects all health authorities to consider the opportunities for co-operative ventures as part of their regular reviews of performance.

PART FIVE: THE HEALTH SERVICE
            IN SCOTLAND, WALES AND
            NORTHERN IRELAND

CHAPTER 10

INTRODUCTION

10.1 Scotland enjoys high standards of health care available to all regardless of income. The proposals in this White Paper will build on these and on a proud tradition of medical and nursing education. Among the achievements published in "The Scottish Health Service" last November were longer life expectancy; fewer still-births; lower rates of perinatal and infant mortality; more in-patients, day cases and out-patient attendances; increased numbers of patients receiving renal dialysis, kidney transplant operations, and operations to replace joints and treat cataracts. There has been progress too in reducing in-patient waiting lists, increasing care for the elderly in their homes, increasing numbers of doctors and nurses and raising the level of the Health Service building programme. Total expenditure in the NHS in Scotland has risen by over 33 per cent in real terms from £1,053 million in 1979-80 to a planned £2,755 million in 1989-90.

10.2 The means of achieving further improvements in the efficient delivery of health care set out in this White Paper apply fully to Scotland. Scotland will maintain its high standards of medical care, the benefits of greater patient choice, modernised and improved buildings and equipment, and a service which is responsive to the needs and wishes of individual patients. The necessary changes can be brought about only by giving staff a more satisfying measure of responsibility coupled with clearer accountability for the results they are expected to produce. This applies not only in hospitals but also in the community and family practitioner services which normally provide the first contact patients have with doctors and nurses.

PUTTING PATIENTS FIRST

10.3 Better patient care is the primary aim of the review. A key element in how patients view the hospital service is the waiting time for treatment, and there is no doubt that many people are still having to wait too long. The Government has already asked Health Boards to reduce the time patients have to wait for hospital treatment, and the increased funds made available for this purpose over the past two years have paid for such things as 175 extra hip replacement operations in Highland and 1,200 extra orthopaedic out-patient consultations in Greater Glasgow. In 1989-90 up to £7 million will be available to Health Boards to continue this work.

10.4 Health Boards will now be asked specifically:

- to plan and deliver their services in a way which aims to meet the expressed wishes of patients;

- to provide hospital and clinic appointment times that patients can rely on;

- to provide clear and helpful leaflets for patients;

- to work towards ensuring that all out-patients are seen by a consultant on their first visit, rather than by a junior doctor;

- to treat patients as valued customers and to ensure that any complaints are handled promptly and sensitively.

The Secretary of State will be considering further how to ensure that Health Boards seek and act upon their patients' views.

PRIMARY HEALTH CARE

10.5 Primary health care services are just that: family doctors, dentists, chemists, opticians, community nurses and health visitors are normally the first point of contact between patients and the Health Service. Responsiveness to patients' needs was a key element in the White Paper on improving primary health care services - "Promoting Better Health". Its detailed implementation is currently being discussed with the professions concerned and Scottish interests are fully represented. The Government believes that primary health care providers should improve their service to patients by better management of their own activities and better co-ordination with those of the hospital service. The Government intends to build on the proposals in the White Paper on primary health care services by:

- encouraging GPs to take more responsibility for the resources they use;

- pressing ahead with plans to let patients have more information about GP services and to make it easier for them to change their doctor;

- increasing competition among GPs by raising the portion of their pay which is related to the number of patients on their lists from 46 per cent to at least 60 per cent as soon as possible, while safeguarding the position of doctors in the less populated areas in Scotland;

- encouraging more economical drug prescribing by giving Health Boards reasonable budgets for their expenditure on drugs, and giving GP practices indicative budgets for their prescribing costs.

10.6 In considering how these changes can best be made, the Government has reviewed the arrangements under which Health Boards run not only the hospitals but also the community health and family practitioner services. This integration has worked well since 1974 and still seems appropriate for Scotland, given the scale of the Health Service and the distribution of population served by each Health Board. The present framework will therefore be retained, but Health Boards will obviously have to make adjustments to give the increased emphasis to accountability and patient choice proposed in this White Paper.

10.7 In Scotland, as elsewhere in the UK, general practitioners should have more freedom to manage the resources which pay for the health care of their patients. Large group practices will be able to choose to have their own budgets from which to buy a range of operations and treatments for their patients, such as hip replacements and cataract removals, direct from whichever hospital can best provide them. These budgets will cover the spread of out-patient services, tests and in-patient treatments described in chapter 6, improvements to premises, the costs of prescribing drugs, and the 70 per cent of the cost of employing practice staff already paid by the Government.

10.8 Health Boards administer family practitioner, hospital and community services, and so should be well placed to run such a scheme. But they will need adequate information systems for the purpose, as will the general practices. GPs who wish to have practice budgets will have to demonstrate to the Health Board that they are capable of managing them, but they will be able to appeal to the Secretary of State against refusal or withdrawal of authorisation. GPs will have the financial freedom and flexibility within these budgets described in chapter 6.

10.9 At first, practices with lists of at least 11,000 patients will be eligible to opt for GP budgets. This represents about sixty practices in Scotland or 5 per cent of the total, a smaller proportion than in England since Scottish list sizes are smaller than average because of the more scattered population. Smaller practices in Scotland will however be able to group together if they wish to do so in order to opt for GP practice budgets; and once some experience has been gained the option could in any event be extended to smaller practices. Details of the scheme will be set out in a working paper which is being published following the review, and the Government will work out suitable arrangements with the Health Boards in whose areas group practices opt for these budgets.

MEDICAL AUDIT

10.10 Medical audit is a fundamental principle of the review. Briefly, it is the systematic process by which doctors continually assess and evaluate their clinical practice, the organisation of services, their managerial function and educational activities. Doctors and managers require such information to enable improvements to be made in services to patients, to plan ahead, and to improve quality. It enables an efficient and effective use to be made of resources.

10.11 It is doctors, not politicians or managers, who treat patients and the Government is therefore seeking the full co-operation of the profession. There have already been consultations on audit with Scottish medical educational interests, including the Royal Colleges, the Universities, the Health Boards, the British Medical Association and the Scottish Council for Postgraduate Medical Education; and the Secretary of State will produce a working paper shortly. Pioneering work by doctors in Lothian has demonstrated how they can examine the effectiveness of clinical care and take steps to improve their own performance.

10.12 Medical audit in primary health care will make use of the micro-computer software already issued free to general practitioners on request - the General Practitioner Administration System for Scotland (G-PASS). This system already assists with repeat prescribing, patient administration, recording details of illness, and the call-and-recall of patients for screening and inoculation. Future versions will help to record information about the outcome of treatments given to patients. Over a third of practices, spread all over Scotland, now use G-PASS. The Government intends to extend its availability to all GPs who use a micro-computer and to make sure it fits in easily with the information systems being developed for the hospital service.

10.13 Another pilot project in Lothian, which the Government plans to extend to an increasing number of general practitioners, provides information on the properties, effects and costs of modern medicines. An interactive viewdata system (VADIS) gives doctors and pharmacists clinical and pharmaceutical information on a wide range of commonly used and new drugs and comparative costs of drugs with the same therapeutic properties. Future developments could give doctors information about their own prescribing costs, with comparisons of local and national averages, and the cost of alternative products. In time, GPs should be able to call up on a visual display screen on their desk information about medicines and about hospital waiting lists so that their patients can be given right away the best obtainable immediate treatment plus information about any subsequent hospital referrals which may be necessary. This should reduce the anxiety and inconvenience which any illness and its treatment inevitably bring.

10.14 There are occasionally reports of alleged over-prescribing by GPs and machinery exists to investigate such cases in the interests of patients and of containing the costs of the Health Service. The Government proposes to make these arrangements more effective, and will consult the profession about changes in the respective roles of Health Boards and area medical committees to make sure that a more obviously impartial judgement can be made in each case.

SELF-GOVERNING HOSPITALS

10.15 The proposals for self-governing hospitals set out in chapter 3 will make a significant contribution to improving services to patients. In the absence of a regional tier in the Scottish Health Service, the Scottish Home and Health Department will be responsible for guiding and supporting those hospitals which meet the criteria, and want to become self-governing, to achieve this status. Subject to legislation, at least two major acute hospitals might attain self-governing status not later than 1992; but in the longer term some 30 Scottish hospitals might be regarded as potential candidates. The Secretary of State will consult interested parties on the implementation of these proposals.

CENTRAL MANAGEMENT OF SCOTTISH HEALTH CARE

10.16 Following the successful introduction of general management, the Government now aims to develop and to strengthen the role of general managers by delegating to them more decision-making on operational matters. Ministers will retain full responsibility for strategic policy and for ensuring the cost-effective use of public money. Delegation downwards must be matched by accountability upwards. General managers are already formally accountable for the spending of their Boards. Building on existing monitoring of progress, the Government will introduce an annual round of accountability reviews and target-setting at which each Health Board will discuss with the Scottish

Home and Health Department the Board's performance over the past year and will agree targets for the coming year.

10.17 The responsibility for health service policy will continue to rest with the Scottish Home and Health Department, reporting to the Minister for Education and Health and the Secretary of State. However, it is desirable that the management of the Health Service should be strengthened and the Government has decided to appoint a Chief Executive for the NHS in Scotland. The Chief Executive will be responsible for the efficiency and performance of the Health Service and for the overall supervision of the execution of policy. He will have responsibility for the establishment of appropriate and adequate information and data systems required to ensure effective delivery of patient services.

10.18 The Scottish Health Service Policy Board will, however, be abolished. In the initial stages, following its launch in 1985, the Board contributed substantially to the work of introducing general management to the Scottish Health Service. Over the last two years, however, it has met infrequently because broad issues of policy can be dealt with more effectively by Ministers directly, seeking advice as necessary through meetings with representatives of Health Boards and other bodies and, in future, through the work of the Advisory Council which will replace the present Health Service Planning Council.

10.19 The decision to replace the Planning Council has been taken in the light of responses to a widely circulated consultation document which sought to establish how best to respond to the changing needs of the Health Service. The Secretary of State will appoint to the new Advisory Council individuals representing Health Service management, professional and other staff, the universities, the private health sector, and other related interests. This will provide the best advice available to the Secretary of State on the exercise of his health functions from people who can provide a range of skills and experience of every aspect of providing modern health care. The Council will also, with his agreement, offer guidance on good practice to Health Boards and others delivering health care. Further details of the composition of the new Council and its committees will be announced, and the necessary legislation prepared, in due course.

10.20 The role of Health Boards has already begun to change with the advent of general management. Their future membership should reflect and assist this process. In particular, general managers should sit on Boards as members. Greater emphasis on the role of Health Boards in commissioning, contracting for, and purchasing services from providers (rather than, as now, supplying most services at their own hand) will make it particularly valuable to have members with business skills and experience on Boards. In future Boards will be somewhat smaller than the present range of 14-22 members and their composition will reflect the changing requirements, with members appointed on the basis of the personal contribution which they can make.

FINANCE

10.21 Money for the current expenditure of the Health Service in Scotland is distributed to the 15 Health Boards according to the Scottish Health Authorities Revenue Equalisation formula (SHARE). This measures the relative needs of the different areas by weightings for the age and sex structure of the population and its morbidity (as indicated by standardised mortality rates).

10.22 The Government proposes to simplify the formula by removing central adjustments for cross-boundary flows. In future the money will follow the patient across Health Board boundaries, so that wherever patients are examined, tested or treated, the Board where the patient lives will pay for the work done by the Board where the work is carried out.

10.23 This change will require prices to be set for a wide range of hospital and laboratory procedures. To begin with, an indicative tariff for acute hospital procedures, based upon their classification into diagnosis-related groups (DRGs) may be set centrally; but in due course providers should be able to set their own prices. The Secretary of State will consult interested bodies during 1989 about what modifications to SHARE might be introduced in 1990-91.

10.24 Considerable further investment in computers and information technology will be needed to produce accurately costed, patient-based, information. Once an accurate information base is available, however, it may be possible to move away from the SHARE formula altogether and to reimburse providers entirely on the basis of work done rather than on the basis of a forecast of needs.

10.25 The Government believes that more managerial freedom will produce a better Health Service for patients. One of the ways of helping the process of change is through the increasing value for money work carried out by those who audit the accounts of the health authorities. This work is currently done by the Scottish Office Audit Unit, which is not part of the Scottish Home and Health Department but is answerable to the Secretary of State. The audits of two Health Boards have recently been contracted out to commercial auditors. The Secretary of State will keep these arrangements under review in order to ensure that they are still the best and most effective means of securing value for money in the Health Service in Scotland.

THE PRIVATE SECTOR

10.26 Scotland's growing independent health sector has 7,000 beds. Most of them give nursing and convalescent care to frail elderly people. In fact, a third of Scotland's long-stay beds are in the private sector. Health Boards already draw on this resource - over 800 nursing home places are taken by NHS patients. Many other residents have their fees paid through social security funds. Nursing homes can offer the very elderly - a fast growing group - congenial surroundings, nursing care, and a choice of location. The Government expects them to play a big part in providing services for the very elderly and, with that in mind, has just made new regulations, to be backed shortly by guidelines of good practice, to promote standards of care. Scotland's voluntary sector - which has already made a large contribution to hospice care - also has an important part to play.

10.27 More Scots are looking to the private sector for the diagnosis and treatment of their health problems. Over the last year, private hospitals have worked closely with the NHS to tackle waiting lists for operations like hip surgery, and cooperation should continue and expand. With the introduction of GP practice budgets, general practitioners in Scotland should be able to choose, if they wish, to buy operations for their NHS patients directly from private hospitals or from self-governing NHS hospitals. The results should be shorter waiting times for operations, and more choice for patients.

10.28 Medical procedures, like renal dialysis, could also benefit from private sector involvement, and Health Boards in Scotland are already looking at how private companies might help them to provide more, and more convenient, dialysis places.

CONCLUSION

10.29 The Government is determined to build on the achievements of the Health Service by making it more responsive to the needs and wishes of individual patients. Following this review patients will have more freedom in choosing their general practitioner and in deciding where they should go for hospital treatment. They will be able to exercise a preference for general practices and hospitals which treat them quickly, courteously and effectively. The changes will require staff to have more responsibility and clearer accountability for their work; and the Government has every confidence that they will respond fully to the new challenges and opportunities ahead. This applies not only in hospitals but also in the community and family practitioner services. Through the means described in this chapter the Government will seek to ensure that the large amounts of money already spent on the Health Service in Scotland are even better managed and are channelled towards those who can provide the best quality of patient care in the most efficient way.

CHAPTER 11

INTRODUCTION

11.1 The people of Wales will benefit fully from the improvements which will flow from the review, and which will make the NHS more responsive to the needs of patients. There are distinctive health care needs and circumstances in Wales. This chapter describes these and the distinctive programme of action for the Principality.

11.2 These improvements will build on the remarkable record of achievement of the NHS in Wales over the last decade. NHS expenditure for an average family of four in Wales has risen from under £11 a week in 1978-79 to the record level of nearly £36 planned for 1989-90, a rise of over 42 per cent in real terms. This has made possible the highest ever number of front line staff. By 1987 there were 327 more hospital, medical and dental staff than in 1979 - an increase of nearly 18 per cent - and 4,733 more nursing and midwifery staff - a real increase of 13 per cent (ie after allowing for the reduction in the standard working hours for nurses). Over £600 million (at 1988-89 prices) has been spent since 1978-79 on new and improved hospitals and other health service facilities. Most important of all, record numbers of patients are receiving the treatment they need: comparing 1987 with 1979, over 99,000 more in-patients were treated (up over 28 per cent); over 88,000 more new out-patients (up over 20 per cent); and over 45,000 more day cases (up nearly 150 per cent). Additional and recurrent Welsh Office investment (£13.75 million in 1988-89) has made possible an unprecedented expansion of community services for those with mental handicaps, at the same time as improvements in the hospitals. Mental illness services are receiving similar recurrent additional investment (over £10 million in 1988-89).

11.3 There is no regional health authority in Wales. Some of the functions of the Regional Health Authorities in England - such as the holding of medical consultants' contracts - are the responsibility of District Health Authorities in the Principality. Others are carried out on authorities' behalf by the Welsh Health Common Services Authority (WHCSA), and there is the special remit of the Health Promotion Authority for Wales, which works in co-operation with the DHAs and other interests, to prevent ill health and promote better health.

11.4 Other regional functions, such as determining the capacity, location and funding of regional services (such as renal dialysis), resource allocation, regional manpower planning, and strategic investment in information systems and technologies, are the direct responsibility of the NHS Directorate in the Welsh Office. The NHS in Wales works under the strategic direction of the Health Policy Board, which is chaired by the Secretary of State. An Executive Committee of the Board is led by the Director of the NHS in Wales and is responsible for carrying into effect the decisions of the Board. The Director is also the Chairman of WHCSA. These arrangements, which were introduced following the NHS management inquiry of 1983, have proved their worth and will continue. They will be focused to ensure the delivery of the programme of action described in this chapter.

PUTTING THE PATIENT FIRST: THE PROGRAMME FOR ACTION

Increased autonomy for hospitals

11.5 The introduction of general management at all levels of the NHS in Wales has already brought a significantly improved focus on quality of care and cost-effectiveness. Unit general managers have been appointed to run hospitals and community services at local level and given clear responsibility, working in co-operation with medical, nursing and professional staffs, for budgets and results. Wales is in the vanguard of the UK-wide drive to introduce the information systems and technologies which are needed to show what individual medical treatments cost.

11.6 The managerial autonomy of hospitals will be further enhanced and hospital management and clinical staff will be given direct responsibility for the services they provide. They will move as quickly as possible to a position where they are, in effect, contracted to provide a given level, range and quality of service.

11.7 It will be possible by the early 1990s for a major acute hospital that so desires to become self-governing, provided that it shows clearly that it will have the capacity to provide efficiently and effectively an adequate range and depth of services to the population it serves. During the 1990s, a wider range of Welsh hospitals might be regarded as potential candidates for self-government, providing the Secretary of State is satisfied that they can carry out the functions required of them.

Widening the choice of health care

11.8 These changes in the management of hospitals will take place against a general background of widening choice of health care.

11.9 Private sector hospital care is relatively poorly developed in Wales, with just 215 in-patient beds. And there are just 54 pay beds in NHS hospitals. These facilities will need to expand to increase patient choice.

11.10 Health authorities in Wales have begun to purchase private sector care where this represents the best deal for patients. These initiatives will be built on to lead a sustained drive to reduce waiting times. Special consideration will be given to the establishment of treatment centres to ensure the rapid turn-round of cases, with direct referrals by GPs for key disabling conditions where waiting times are too long, such as hip and knee replacements, cataracts, varicose veins and hernias.

11.11 The drive to widen choice in health care for the benefit of patients will be supported and encouraged by changes in the way in which resources are allocated. Money must move with the patient so that hospitals which are efficient and effective, and attract more work, get the resources they need. Detailed proposals will be the subject of consultation.

Assuring quality of care

11.12 The Welsh Office will work jointly with the other UK Health Departments and the professions to introduce as rapidly as possible a comprehensive system of medical audit. There will be close working with the professions and the representative bodies in Wales to build on the work which has already been done. The NHS in Wales will embark upon a programme to improve the quality of acute care and other services, commencing with proposals in 1989 for better ways to inform patients about services and to take account of patients' views in the development of services.

Additional consultants

11.13 Between 1982 and 1987 there was an increase of 118, or 18 per cent, in the whole-time equivalent number of medical and dental consultants in Wales. Six further posts will be created over the next three years. These will be in addition to the posts being created under the "Achieving a Balance" initiative.

Closer involvement of doctors in management

11.14 Wales is well advanced in developing the role of clinicians in management, in particular through the pilot resource management project and the development of costings for individual treatments. This work will be accelerated, so that information systems to enable doctors to work with general managers and ensure the most cost-effective use of resources are in place throughout Wales by 1992.

Developing the role of the GP

11.15 The NHS in Wales has taken the lead in encouraging the closer involvement of GPs in the planning and development of hospital services, through an experiment under which the decisions of GPs about where patients receive hospital treatment will be reflected in the DHA's planning and budgeting. The experience gained will be used to develop the role of GPs in service planning across Wales.

11.16 There is already a sustained drive to equip GPs with the management systems and technologies they need to make effective referrals to hospital services. The central elements are information about waiting lists, waiting times and the costs of treatment. This programme will be accelerated so that by 1992 all GPs in Wales will have up-to-date information on which to base their decisions.

11.17 As these initiatives take effect, and as GPs are able to demonstrate their management capacity in these new ways, the programme to enable GPs to hold budgets for their expenditure, and those of key areas of hospital services, will be extended to Wales. At first, practices with lists of at least 11,000 will be eligible to apply to hold budgets; this represents about 30 practices in Wales. Details of the scheme will be set out in a working paper which the Secretary of State will publish as soon as possible. Subject to suitable arrangements being worked out with the appropriate health authorities, the Government would like to see a number of GP budgets in operation by the early 1990s.

Promoting better health

11.18 There is far too much avoidable illness and premature death in Wales. Levels of coronary heart disease, strokes and most forms of cancer are significantly higher in Wales than on average in the UK. A sustained drive to tackle these problems is central to the future of a prosperous Wales. The Secretary of State has set up the Health Promotion Authority for Wales to lead this drive, building on the success of Heartbeat Wales. Detailed proposals for action will be published later this year.

The health authorities

11.19 Health authority memberships will be reconstructed with the creation of new style boards on which the non-executive members, including the chairman, will be appointed by the Secretary of State. There will be a strong emphasis in these appointments on leadership and top level management qualities. The Secretary of State will continue to appoint at least one member to each authority in Wales from the University of Wales College of Medicine. The executive directors of each board will include the district general manager and the medical, nursing and finance directors. The non-executive directors will form a majority.

11.20 The new boards will sharpen the focus on the delivery of cost-effective services and the quality of care, through the development of the DHAs' role as enablers and purchasers of services, rather than simply as direct providers.

The Family Practitioner Committees

11.21 The Family Practitioner Committees (FPCs) have major leadership and management tasks, which are taken further by the proposals in this White Paper. They too will therefore have newly structured memberships, along the lines set out in chapter 7. Each FPC in Wales will have a chief executive, selected by the Committee following open competition, who will be a member of the Committee.

The consumer voice

11.22 There are 22 Community Health Councils (CHCs) in Wales. Their memberships come from the voluntary sector, the local authorities, and by direct appointment by the Secretary of State. In the light of the new style boards of DHAs, there is a strong case for their being one CHC for each DHA area, to represent the consumer voice in a clear and more focused way. The Secretary of State will publish proposals along these lines for consultation.

Value for money

11.23 All of these proposals are aimed to secure better patient care and to see that the maximum benefit is obtained from the large resources that will be available. To help authorities achieve targets for cost improvement programmes and the generation of income, a value for money unit will be set up in the NHS Directorate. There will be increased emphasis on independent value for money studies. To help secure this the external audit of the NHS in Wales will become the responsibility of the Audit Commission.

CHAPTER 12

THE ACHIEVEMENTS OF THE SERVICE

12.1 The people of Northern Ireland already enjoy a high standard of health care. Hospital and other health facilities throughout the Province have a well-deserved reputation for responding to needs across the whole community, ranging from the provision of complex regional services at major centres of excellence such as the Royal Group of hospitals, to the continuing care of elderly people. The majority of family doctors practise from health centres in association with primary care staff. The combined planning and management of health and personal social services have brought real advantages in continuity of care.

12.2 Recent years have seen substantial enhancements in services and improvements in efficiency. Since 1978 funding for the health services in Northern Ireland has increased in real terms by almost 30 per cent; there are 20 per cent more doctors and 13 per cent more nurses employed than ten years ago. Annual hospital admissions have grown by 15 per cent to over 210,000 and almost 30,000 people now receive treatment annually as day cases. There have been major developments in regional services: the kidney transplant programme in Belfast is recognised as being the most successful in the UK, and important medical advances have been achieved in other fields such as mobile coronary care and neurosurgery. In the family practitioner services, major initiatives aimed at promoting more cost-effective prescribing have brought about substantial savings in the Province's drug bill.

12.3 These major improvements could not have been achieved without the continuing commitment of staff at all levels. But there is clear scope for improving the quality and promptness of the service that patients receive, and the efficiency with which scarce and expensive resources are used. The proposals in this White Paper will be applied in Northern Ireland to achieve these aims within the objectives of the Government's health strategy for the Province.

KEY CHANGES

12.4 The Government's principal objective is to show real improvements in service for every patient. This will involve:

- delegating as much power and responsibility as possible to the local level, including the appointment of unit general managers in major acute hospitals and the reorganisation of the management of the major teaching hospitals in Belfast;

- engaging doctors in the management of the services and obtaining their commitment to medical audit;

- encouraging some hospitals to progress towards self-governing status as Hospital Trusts;

- encouraging larger GP practices to opt for their own budgets for buying particular services direct from hospitals;

- reconstituting Health and Social Services Boards as management bodies;

- developing a simpler system for resource allocation which will fund Boards for the populations they serve rather than the services they provide;

- strengthening arrangements for the external audit of the services to ensure better value for money.

SERVICE TO PATIENTS

12.5 These key changes must be accompanied by the pursuit of clinical excellence, as well as a desire to treat patients as people. Sometimes the service is too impersonal and inflexible and the patient's sense of vulnerability may be heightened by a failure to give clear and sensitive explanations of what is happening. The Government is determined to enhance the quality of the care provided to patients by encouraging:

- the publication of guides to the services available in individual hospitals and GP practices;

- the establishment of appointment systems which give people individual appointment times which they can rely on;

- the publication of information on expected waiting times for first appointments, diagnostic tests and in-patient treatment;

- the provision of a wide range of optional extras and amenities for patients who are prepared to pay for them;

- the establishment of straightforward procedures for making suggestions for improvements and, if necessary, complaints;

- the provision of quiet and pleasant waiting areas with proper counselling facilities;

- the rapid notification of the results of diagnostic tests.

| MORE EFFECTIVE MANAGEMENT |

12.6 There have been General Managers in the Boards at area level since 1985, while units are still managed by unit management groups. Boards have recently completed detailed management audits which show that further decision-making should be devolved to the local level.

12.7 The Government believes that management at local level would now support, and to be fully effective requires, the appointment of unit general managers in major acute hospitals. These complex institutions increasingly need a management focus capable of securing the co-operation and support of the various professional groups on whom the successful implementation of effective change depends.

12.8 Similarly, the Government believes that the management of the major Belfast teaching hospitals requires to be brought together and strengthened to ensure their complementary working. It therefore supports the development of a unified management structure for these hospitals within the Eastern Board.

12.9 Boards will now be asked to review their management structures generally and to submit proposals.

HOSPITAL CONSULTANTS

12.10 The Government welcomes the increasing willingness of hospital consultants to assume managerial responsibility. It wishes to extend and strengthen medical participation in management so that the profession can contribute more effectively to decision-making and so influence the future direction of the services. To this end, the Government is providing financial and technical support for resource management initiatives which are under way at the Royal Victoria and Tyrone County Hospitals, and will be extending such systems to all major hospitals.

12.11 The Government wishes to see all hospital doctors in Northern Ireland participating in medical audit, through peer review. Discussion will take place with the medical profession over the introduction of an effective system of medical audit which will critically review the quality and effectiveness of medical care provided to patients.

12.12 Within the national framework to be developed between the Government and the medical profession, Health and Social Services Boards will be asked to agree a fuller job description for each of their consultants. It is also intended to change appointment procedures for consultants to enable General Managers to participate in the process. This will help ensure that the successful candidate meets the requirements of the post for the management of resources and the development of services. Parallel changes to those in Great Britain will be made to disciplinary procedures and the distinction awards system.

SELF -GOVERNING HOSPITALS

12.13 The introduction of unit general managers in major acute hospitals will facilitate progress towards self-governing status for a small number of hospitals by 1992. The same conditions for self-governing status will apply as elsewhere in the UK, and similar management arrangements will be needed.

12.14 It will be necessary for hospitals to demonstrate the existence of a settled management structure, involving senior professional staff. Improved information systems for both management and clinical purposes and a widespread system of medical audit will be required. Self-governing hospitals will continue to provide essential core services to their local population including accident and emergency services. There will be appropriate linkages to services in the community in order to ensure continuity of care. Self-governing hospitals will also, where appropriate, undertake necessary teaching and research activities. Effective safeguards will prevent any self-governing hospital abusing its position as a monopoly supplier.

THE FAMILY PRACTITIONER

12.15 GPs have a key part to play in maintaining the health of the population and ensuring that hospital services are used appropriately. Patients look to their GP for advice and to provide access to specialised services, and their role needs to be strengthened to make these services more responsive to patients' needs. Improved information systems will be required, including information on hospital waiting lists and GP referral patterns.

12.16 There are proportionately fewer general practices in Northern Ireland large enough to opt for a practice budget, but the Government is keen to encourage and facilitate those which wish to take this course. Enhanced information systems and training programmes will be needed for general practices which wish to hold their own budgets and could be in place in the early 1990s.

12.17 The other proposals in this White Paper in respect of the family practitioner services will be implemented through the local structures in Northern Ireland. These include the development of medical audit in general practice, the encouragement of greater competition with better information and streamlining of procedures for changing GP, and changes in payment structures and in the retirement age. The Government will continue to support a programme of computerisation in general practice, which will itself help to enhance the quality and effectiveness of the care provided.

12.18 The Government also intends to arrange for Health and Social Services Boards to be given budgets to cover the prescribing costs of practices in their areas, and in turn to give indicative budgets to individual practices. This will be the subject of local consultation with the professions and other interests.

12.19 In parallel, the Government will continue with its existing initiatives to improve primary care services in the Province, including the greater involvement of GPs in the delivery of co-ordinated health and social services at the local level.

MEMBERSHIP OF HEALTH AND SOCIAL SERVICES BOARDS

12.20 Boards will be reconstituted as management bodies on similar lines to NHS authorities in Great Britain. District Councils and professional organisations will thus no longer be represented on the Boards, but will have a continuing voice in an advisory and consultative capacity. The present District Committees have a limited remit and a highly localised focus. The Government intends to replace them by four Area Committees, one relating to each Board, with stronger advisory and consultative powers and representation largely from District Councils and voluntary interests.

FINANCIAL MANAGEMENT

12.21 The Government intends to replace the present formula for calculating target revenue allocations by a simpler system, as in Great Britain. The adoption of the new system will require better and more timely information on the extent and cost to each Board of treating patients, including the cost of cross-boundary patient flows. In essence, each Board will be funded on a capitation basis, weighted to reflect the health and age distribution of the population, to secure services for its resident population, and to pay for services in its own or other hospitals. There will be separate funding for teaching and research, and the new arrangements will need to be introduced on a carefully phased basis.

12.22 The Government intends to strengthen existing arrangments for the external audit of the health and personal social services, including the greater use of the private sector, to ensure better value for money.

CONCLUSION

12.23 One of the major themes of the current Regional Strategy for the Health and Personal Social Services in Northern Ireland is to encourage members of the public to assume greater responsibility for maintaining their own health. At the same time, when ill-health strikes, it is essential that individuals should receive treatment which is fully responsive to their needs and of the highest possible quality. The best way to ensure this is to place more choice in the hands of individual patients and to shift responsibility, as far as possible, to those who are in a position directly to satisfy the needs of patients. Better use of resources will in turn speed up the achievement of the objectives of the strategy. The proposals in this White Paper will be effective in achieving these aims no less in Northern Ireland than in England, Scotland or Wales.

PART SIX: CONCLUSION

CHAPTER 13

INTRODUCTION

13.1 The proposals in this White Paper put the interests and wishes of the patient first. They offer a new, exciting and potentially rewarding challenge to all who work in the NHS. They add up to the most significant review of the NHS in its 40-year history. And they amount to a formidable programme of reform which will require energy and commitment to carry it through.

13.2 The Government is planning to implement the programme in three main phases:

Phase 1: 1989

The Secretary of State for Health will establish a new NHS Policy Board and reconstitute the NHS Management Board as a Management Executive.

The Health Departments, and Regional Health Authorities (RHAs) in England, will identify the first hospitals to become self-governing as NHS Hospital Trusts, and plan for their new status; will devolve further operational responsibility to Districts and hospitals; and will begin preparing the ground for GP practice budgets.

The Government will introduce Regulations to make it easier for patients to change their GPs.

The first additional consultant posts will be created; Districts will begin agreeing job descriptions with their consultants; and a new framework for medical audit will begin to be implemented.

The resource management initiative will be extended to more major acute hospitals.

Preparations for indicative drug budgets for GPs will begin.

The Audit Commission will begin its work in the NHS.

Phase 2: 1990

The changes begun in Phase 1 will gather momentum. Devolving operational responsibility, changing the management of consultants' contracts and extending medical audit throughout the hospital service will near completion.

"Shadow" boards of the first group of NHS Hospital Trusts will start to develop their plans for the future.

RHAs, District Health Authorities (DHAs) and Family Practitioner Committees (FPCs) will be reconstituted, and FPCs will become accountable to RHAs. Regions will begin paying directly for work they do for each other.

Phase 3: 1991

The first NHS Hospital Trusts will be established.

The first GP practice budget-holders will begin buying services for their patients.

The indicative drug budget scheme will be implemented.

DHAs will begin paying directly for work they do for each other.

13.3 The reforms in this White Paper will enable a higher quality of patient care to be obtained from the resources which the nation is able to devote to the NHS. The provision for spending on health in the coming financial year, 1989-90, announced in the Autumn Statement, included the likely costs of preparing for the reforms and for the legislation which will give effect to them. Over time, any extra costs should be offset by the improved efficiency which will stem from them. The total provision for spending on health will take account of the progress made in implementing the reforms - including the increased efficiency savings. The costs of implementing the reforms in future years will be considered as part of the annual public expenditure surveys.

13.4 A number of the changes proposed will require legislation, which will be introduced at the earliest opportunity.

13.5 Throughout this programme, the Government will hold to its central aims: to extend patient choice, to delegate responsibility to those who are best placed to respond to patients' needs and wishes, and to secure the best value for money. The result will be a better deal for the public, both as patients and as taxpayers. The Government will build further on the strengths of the NHS, while tackling its weaknesses. This will ensure that the NHS becomes an even stronger, more modern Service, more committed than ever to working for patients.

Printed in the UK for HMSO
Dd. 5061097   C25   8/93   51–4136   4073   Ord. 256183